Writer in the Library!

41 Writers Reveal How They Use Libraries
to Develop Their Skill, Craft & Careers

by
Lee McQueen

1st Edition

McQueen ♟ Press
Chicago, Illinois

Published by McQueen Press
info@mcqueenpress.com
www.mcqueenpress.com

About the Author
Lee McQueen has been a librarian and bookstore owner. With a Master of Library & Information Science from SUNY-Buffalo, she indexes and abstracts and takes on research, writing, and database assignments. She has also written biographical articles, essays, a novel, short stories, poems, biographical articles, and screenplays.

"Maple Valley Branch Library, 1967" *On the Bus with Rosa Parks,* W.W. Norton & Co., Inc., © 1999 by Rita Dove. Reprinted by permission of the author, Rita Dove.

Original essay written in 2006 for *Writer in the Library!* Used with permission of the author, Rudolfo Anaya.

Cover design, interior design, and typesetting by Lee McQueen.

Logo is a registered mark of McQueen Press and should not be copied without permission.

McQueen, Lee
Writer in the Library! 41 Writers Reveal How They Use Libraries to Develop Their Skill, Craft & Careers /Lee McQueen – 1st Edition

ISBN 978-0-9798515-4-4 (pbk)

Dedicated to Artists of the Written Word
…and to the Libraries Who Love Them

Available at McQueen Press

Short Story Collections

Imaginarium

The Dark Fantastic

Poetry Collection

Things I Forgot to Tell You

Novels

Kenzi

Jeannie East, then West

Screenplays

The Angel and the Lion

Kindred

"There is, in fact, no subject to which a member of Congress
may not have occasion to refer." Thomas Jefferson

Table of Contents

Preface *i*

Chapter 1
Why Are Writers in the
Libraries? *3*

Chapter 2
Novelists & Short Story
Writers
Anaya, Rudolfo *11*
Carman, Patrick *12*
Edens, Cooper *14*
Foglio, Phil *16*
Jance, J.A. *18*
McFarlane, Sheryl *20*
McGee, Anthony Ellis *22*
Moore, Terry *24*
Nance, John *26*
Olshan, Matthew *30*
Ufer, David *33*
Williams, Suzanne *35*

Chapter 3
Poets & Lyricists
Dove, Rita *39*
Gegic, Dave *41*
Lansana, Quraysh Ali *44*
Niño, Raúl *48*
Plumpp, Sterling D. *50*
Rivera, Louis Reyes *53*
Smith, Marc Kelly *57*

Chapter 4
Playwrights & Screenwriters
Diamond, Lydia *63*
Hanley, Kirk *65*
Porter, Matthew *68*
Pritchett, Dylan *70*

Pugh, Libya *74*
Wiley, Mike *76*

Chapter 5
Non-Fiction Writers &
Essayists
Abdul-Aziz, Zaid *83*
Angus, Jeff *86*
Axelrod, Alan *89*
Black Jr., Timuel D. *91*
Buchwald, Claire *94*
Chiffolo, Anthony *97*
Molinary, Rosie *100*
Norfleet, George *103*
Orman, Roscoe *105*
Savage, Jeff *108*
Sterling, Dackeyia *111*

Chapter 6
Academic, Technical &
Professional Writers
Aman, Mohammed *115*
Burgess, John *119*
Hodge, Anthony *122*
Olopade, Olofunmilayo *125*
Pramas, Chris *127*

Chapter 7
Classic Library Quotes
Old School *131*
New School *137*

Appendix
Glossary of Library Terms *143*
Resources *150*
Acknowledgements *152*
Index *154*

Preface

This project began December 2006 when I finally noticed that I'd made extreme use of library resources to research my writing for the past two years. I wondered whether it was just me or whether other writers that I admired and looked up to discovered the same phenomenon in their own careers. If so, then maybe I was on the right track towards the wonderful adventure of writing and publishing. Out of sheer curiosity, I decided to find out.

I decided to focus on North American writers. I used *Contemporary Authors*, a database by the Gale Group with pretty comprehensive information on today's authors making significant contributions in the world of the written word, to begin background research. I also visited the official websites of the writers that had them up and running. I checked *Who's Who in America* which proved useful in locating entries on the remaining authors I didn't find online. My final stop was *Wikipedia*, an online encyclopedia as well as actual publications produced by the writers for additional biographical information.

I sent a call for writers to those with publicly-available mailing addresses (post office boxes, agents, or publishers). I sent the letters with an SASE, setting a 750 word limit, and a two-and-a-half month deadline. This took lots of envelopes, lots of stamps, lots of glue stick, and a little bit of clear tape. Those authors with publicly-available email addresses received advanced notice.

Then I crossed my fingers.

I figured 25% of the letters would be lost, misdirected, or "junked." 25% of the recipients would decline. 25% of the recipients would express interest and then change their minds or forget. This would leave a final 25%.

But that was too easy!

So I attended the American Library Association's Midwinter Meeting in Seattle and Summer Convention in Washington, D.C., plus other book fairs, book signings, and writing events to see if I could catch writers willing to do an interview. I liked the idea of interviews because I'd done author interviews previously and really enjoyed the experience. The writers seemed to enjoy the interviews as well. In fact, they preferred the interviews. This is why nearly every entry is an interview transcript of the answers to the same six questions.

My own answers to those same questions provide an example:

1. Describe your earliest experience as a library user, visitor, patron, or customer.

My earliest experience as a library visitor was accompanying my mother to the university library as she worked towards her sociology degree. It seemed a very important place to me because I knew it was an important place to her. I remember we went there often.

2. How did libraries contribute to your early career as a writer?

I used libraries extensively as a student writing my term papers and I continued to use them when I began writing research articles. Each advance in technology helped me to improve my research.

3. What types of reading materials or books are in your personal book collection or library?

I have many reference books such as dictionaries, thesauri, encyclopedias, manuals, and handbooks.

4. Besides libraries, what other resources do you use to research your writing?

Besides libraries, I use newspapers and conversations with other people for research. People have many stories to share and often those conversations spark a creative response within me.

5. What value do you believe libraries have to the general public?

Libraries document history. Without history, we are a lost people.

6. How have you used libraries for your latest work(s)?

The online databases and reference book sections are extremely helpful.

Just like the materials found in many public and academic libraries, the subjects of the entries cross gender, race, age, political, philosophical, cultural, subject, and genre lines. Three common denominators are that

(1) they were all writers, (2) had something to say about the contribution or influence of libraries on their writing careers, and (3) were willing to participate. I decided to group them in alphabetical order by genre specialties. Some writers routinely cross genres so I had to make the hard decision of where to place them. For instance, a writer known for poetry may also write plays. Several writers with education at the graduate or doctoral level are found in the General Non-Fiction Writers & Essayists section instead of the Academic, Technical & Professional Writers section based upon the type of writing they produce or are most well-known for writing.

This book's primary audience consists of established writers, up and coming writers, librarians, teachers, writing and book industry professionals, as well as fans of particular authors. This book is for the reluctant library user, visitor, patron, or customer as well. Perhaps persons unfamiliar with or uncertain of the whole library experience, specifically in North America, may decide to give these "free bookstores" a try. To that end, the book contains a pretty detailed Index for anyone needing access to specific information as well as the Glossary of Library Terms to explain terminology mentioned by various subjects. Footnotes, photo and image captions, biographies, front matter, Classic Quotes, and back matter are not indexed.

The footnotes found with many of the interviews include terms or references that may not be familiar to persons outside the fields of the interviewee's subject specialty, as well as outside the fields of writing and librarianship. Hopefully, expansion on these terms will create a friendly, educational experience for the reader. Many of these terms were mentioned by multiple writers. In such instances, the footnote is listed where the term is first mentioned by a subject within this book. The footnote is found on the *first* page of mention rather than on each page of mention. So, basically, it's the luck of the draw where the footnotes are found... or, rather, the luck of alphabetical order. The sole exception, I believe, is the term "bookmobile," footnoted twice. For the curious, a review of the Index will quickly show each specific page that a subject mentioned a certain term.

Two similar books released in 2006 are listed in the Bibliography for further perusal. One is *The Book That Changed My Life*. The other is *You've Got to Read This Book!* In both books, many authors and others reveal the way specific books impacted their lives. *Writer in the Library!* reveals how *libraries* with all their accompanying personnel, services, policies, procedures, products, and physical presences affect the overall careers of writers. Another book, *Writer in the Public Library* (1984), discusses writer-in-residence programs, workshops, and writer resource centers within libraries. As I mentioned before, the amazing diversity of backgrounds, genres, even geography meant that although these writers approached their crafts in different ways all roads crossed and circled, doubled back, and tunneled through the library system at one point or another. So for librarians, publishers, and fellow writers, I recommend these books as well to find out what drives the mind of a writer to write, what forks in the road they choose, and what sights they stop to see before they exit to the end destination, The Finished Masterpiece. The Classic Quotes section contains pithy commentary on libraries by writers of both the Old and New Schools. Readers are encouraged share their own commentary on this book or writing and library usage in general with others at http://www.mcqueenpress.com/blog.html.

Writer in the Library! does not provide comprehensive information on libraries, librarians, librarianship, writers, or writing. Instead, it is a complement to many other texts available on these subjects. The reader should read all such available material and then tailor that information to the reader's needs. This text should be used as a general guide, not the ultimate source of information on writing and/or librarianship. The purpose of *Writer in the Library!* is to both educate and entertain.

All opinions stated by individual subjects within this volume remain those of the subject and do not necessarily reflect the opinions of this book's publisher, author, the subject's organization(s), or fellow subjects within this book.

I wish to thank each subject for taking the time to share with readers of *Writer in the Library!* the role that libraries had and still have in making them the writer they were yesterday, are today, and will be tomorrow. Their expertise and ideas were crucial to this first work of reference non-fiction produced by McQueen Press.

And especially, thank you Libraries!

Love,
Lee

Chicago, Illinois
January 2008

Chapter 1

Why are Writers in the Libraries?

Libraries symbolize a reckoning of the past, an attempt to explain the present, and a hope for the future. After all, books are written to be read, songs are sung to be heard, images are documented to be seen, games are meant to be played by... *someone.*

Libraries are lessons learned, often the hard way, and hopefully, the fervent writer may wish, never to be forgotten. Ever.

They are the collected and collective intelligence of a people, a nation, a planet, a world.

Someday, for whatever reason, an alien civilization may review Earth's libraries, television, radio, film, and computers to find the answer to the question of that day. "What is Earth?"

They would likely glean the most information, perhaps the *most reliable* information, from Earth's libraries.

A writer should feel proud.

Earliest Library Experiences

Immediately, the reader of this book will notice the patterns. At a very young age, usually before the age of ten, either the mother or father introduced the writer to the library.

> **"My mother and father, my mother mostly, would take us to the library that was on Grand Boulevard called Forestville." Black**

> **"My mother took us to the library every week." Buchwald**

> **"My earliest experience at going to the library was with my mother when I was probably two or three years old." Burgess**

> **"When I was probably about eight or nine or ten, I can't remember exactly, my mom used to use the public library as a babysitting service." Carman**

> **"In my early years of school, my grandmother, in particular, would introduce me to our local library in the Bronx." Orman**

> **"My first experience with the library that had an effect on me was the fact that my mother was an assistant at the library in my hometown of Virginia." Wiley**

> **"I remember that my parents used to take me and my two sisters and brother to the library every couple of weeks when I grew up in Eugene, Oregon." Williams**

Or, schools introduced the writer to the library.

> **"That would have to be in my high school library where I went to look for a book to do a research paper in physics." Olopade**

> **"The first library experience I really remember is probably when I was in middle school although I don't exactly remember the grade or the age." Chiffolo**

For some writers, library usage became part of the grand adventure of youth.

"We would roller-skate downtown to the main library on Randolph which is now the Cultural Center."
Black

"We dragged our Radio Flyer wagon back and forth loaded with wagon loads of library books." Jance

These future writers sought many things: adventure, fantasy, quiet places and spaces, and sometimes, specific information. Not only did some libraries unwittingly serve as free babysitting or daycare services, libraries also became free community centers, free classrooms, "free bookstores," free shelters from rain and extreme temperatures, and free entertainment.

So while the question of why writers are in the libraries remains, one could also ask the same of astronomers, architects, bus drivers, doctors, drifters, gardeners, the homeless, and lawyers.

"What on earth are you doing in the library?"

Parents, grandparents, guardians, teachers, librarians, and nicely priced (usually free) quality products, we look significantly in your direction.

Early Writing Careers

Just as painters and artists and artisans might view museums and galleries, just as gardeners and farmers might view restaurants and groceries, so might writers and authors view libraries and bookstores. The creator eventually meets the appreciator in a special environment strategically arranged for joyful, ravenous consumption. Maybe the library is a sort of book restaurant, book grocery, or book museum with the most appreciative audience being the creators themselves.

In the following chapters, the reader will see that writers enjoy a unique perspective on the concept of gathering information in order to formulate new information. However, for them, libraries don't just open a world of information. They also open a world of imagination and inspiration.

Personal Libraries of Writers

And writers don't just write. Writers read. They have limitless interests and hobbies and backgrounds – art, photography, music, religion, travel, drawing, history, business, aviation, engineering, crafts, and sports. Therefore, their own libraries may contain materials for entertainment and escape to those other places and spaces. Perhaps this goes back to the childhood glee of taking a break from the rules of life to explore new worlds, realities, adventures, and ideas.

But writers don't just read and write. Writers research! Their personal libraries may also contain materials for reference and information such as encyclopedias, dictionaries, thesauri, handbooks, and style guides.

In addition, personal libraries of writers may contain materials for friends and family to share. Several writers mention that their collections represent the interests of others in their lives, particularly children.

Finally, it is forgivable for a writer to use a shelf, wall unit, or an entire room as a repository for his or her own writing. In fact, there is historical precedent.

"I now have a library of nearly 900 volumes, over 700 of which I wrote myself." Henry David Thoreau

Naturally, the prolific writer would wish to keep track of past writing as a reference and perhaps an inspiration. If I can write *that*, then surely I can write *this*. Or, having one's own books close at hand may serve as a necessary record to keep one's stories (ha, ha) straight.

Resources Other Than Libraries

The groups of writers included in this book distinctly remember using the card catalog as children, teens, and young adults. Most have adapted, along with the rest of the world, to the online catalogs and intranets of the early 1990s as well as web-based catalogs from the mid-1990s forward. Many writers made reference to online research and the use of online stores to purchase research materials.

However, a surprising number of writers admit to the ongoing benefits of interviewing subjects, having general conversations, and interacting with every day people. In addition, many writers mentioned their reliance on the powers of perception and intuition through close observation of their surroundings as a reliable method to gather information.

A recurring theme among some writers and researchers is research technique that addresses the computer versus book question. After all, there's nothing like actually being there. Libraries and/or archives hold rare documents such as maps, diaries, family histories, tax records, and bills of sale often available in original format plus expensive collections of reference works financially prohibitive to the individual researcher. To these writers, the value of research lies in books and print resources.

However, some writers strictly use online resources because the research value lies in currency and convenience. Other writers do not perceive research technique as an all or nothing proposition. In fact, quite a few writers have developed strategies to use both the computer and the book to their advantage finding both general and library-provided resources online. Still others rely neither on computers nor books for information. Instead, they use other resources available to them such as music, film, art, travel, other people, places, or things in order to absorb information.

Or, one can look at it this way.

Legible books printed on tablet, skins, papyrus, linen, and paper remain in existence for hundreds, sometimes thousands of years. Hundreds more years must pass before we know for sure whether computer files will endure as long. Eight-tracks, cassettes, albums, CDs, video, DVDs, and their mechanical or electronic players come and go. The handheld, portable information retrieval system, known as "book," does seem to enjoy a long shelf life with the proper care.

Overall, it is obvious that use of physical books, documents, newspapers and other periodicals, and other print resources plus actual human interaction will never go out of style. However, this type of physical research with tangible materials may be enhanced or supplemented, perhaps even, *supplanted* by computerized research of electronic materials. Recommended for further reading on this research dilemma is *Risen: Why Libraries Are Here to Stay* [see Bibliography].

Libraries and the General Public

Many writers feel that libraries are an under-utilized resource whether for reasons of marketing, access, or an out-dated information delivery system. In addition, libraries face stiff competition for the hearts and minds and souls of a restless customer base. Who hasn't seen someone in a long line at the grocery store elect to read a magazine to pass the time with no intent to purchase? That's a library! Well, okay. Not the best example. But some writers did mention using chain bookstores as libraries.

However, many writers included in this book also agree that libraries level the playing field and serve as great social and educational equalizers. Libraries exist as a type of civic-minded, taxpayer-supported mall of information where a customer can find a "free bookstore" with print, audio, and electronic selections; a free movie rental of documentaries, instructional, and feature films in various formats; and a free music center with popular and classical music in various formats.

But that's not all!

Libraries offer free teen hang-outs, free air-conditioning, free drinking fountains, and free masters-level answers to questions of the day. Everyone who steps inside can feel safe and included, without the cost of admission, a drink minimum, or a 15-20% tip.

Libraries and the Latest Work

For their latest and greatest works, some writers reveal that they consider the library an extension of the library collections in their own homes. Being good neighbors, they agree to share their extended collections with the rest of the world.

Some writers use libraries as a marketing tool - a sort of testing ground. A reading, workshop, or demonstration (with refreshments if attendees are lucky) at the library reaps the reward of instant feedback on and anticipation of new and forthcoming works. Those writers shut out of conglomerate bookstore chains, or who specifically choose not to use chain bookstores do an end run around the cost of doing business and still find access to their audience and the general reading public through libraries.

Referring back to the road analogy from the Preface, for the writer, learning the library's system of organization by call number (the book's address), shelf arrangement (the book's street), and subject area (the book's neighborhood), within the library (the book's city) creates a method to check out the competition to see how their new and forthcoming works measure up to other writers or fill gaps in general knowledge. Interestingly, some writers use their library navigation skills to shop for editors, publishers, graphic artists, illustrators, photographers, and other experts who contribute to the book trade, inside the books of fellow writers.

Finally, according to nearly all of the writers, all roads intersect at atmosphere. The library is excellent therapy for writer's block. Surrounded by shelves filled with the works of old school writers, new school writers see tangible evidence that a blank piece of paper (or a blank computer screen) can become something wonderful with just a turn of the page or a click of the mouse.

> **"You walk through the stacks of a library and you want to be part of it. You want to get yourself in those shelves somewhere." Axelrod**

Medieval Writing Desk

Chapter 2

Novelists
&
Short Story
Writers

Novel – Fictional prose narrative in which characters and situations are depicted within the framework of a plot. Seems as though it could be a factual description of actual people and events, but is not.

Short Story – Work of prose fiction, characterized by brevity and by strictly ordered economy of plot and character.

Rudolfo Anaya

Mary Sundstrom

Rudolfo Anaya is Professor Emeritus of English at the University of New Mexico. Winner of the 2001 National Medal of Arts for literature, he is well-known for the novels, *Bless Me, Ultima; Heart of Aztlan; Shaman Winter*, and the epic poem, *An Elegy on the Death of Cesar Chavez*. His latest work, *Curse of the ChupaCabra* (University of Mexico Press), is an allegorical thriller combining folktale with the modern dilemma of drugs in the youth community.

Original essay written by Rudolfo Anaya for *Writer in the Library!* 2006

As a child, I regularly visited the Santa Rosa, New Mexico Public Library. It was a one room library atop the fire house. I found all sorts of young adult novels to keep me enthralled. Since then I have visited many libraries. I am currently on the Dean's Advisory Board at Zimmerman Library at the University of New Mexico.

My wife and I sponsor an annual lecture, <u>Critica Nueva</u>, at Zimmerman Library. We also sponsor a Chicano Literature annual literary prize, <u>Premio Aztlan</u>, at the library. Libraries are the heart and soul of any community.

Even as we go more and more online for information, libraries still contain the solid stepping stones of civilization. Support your libraries; safeguard civilization.

Patrick Carman

McQueen Press

Carman founded an advertising agency in Portland, OR and designed the *Applause* board game. He built *MyWebPal,* which was the third largest provider of online newspapers. His media production company, Amped Radio, produced and distributed radio and television shows, *The Weekend 22* and *Inside the Music.* Works include "Land of Elyon" fantasies (*The Dark Hills Divide, Beyond the Valley of Thorns, The Tenth City)* and the "Atherton" fantasy series *(House of Power).*

Interview at American Library Association Mid-Winter Meeting. Seattle, WA. 2007

MQPress: Please describe your earliest experience as a library user, visitor, patron, or customer.

Carman: When I was probably about eight or nine or ten, I can't remember exactly, my mom used to use the public library as a babysitting service. We would go up there on Saturdays. She would go look at books and just tell my brother and I to do what we wanted to do. The library became sort of a sacred place because our house was very noisy and loud and I loved going. I have great memories of going to the library. My mom going off to do her own thing and my brother and I going to the kid book area and just spending hours going through the shelves. Finding a corner and just enjoying good books. Great memories of libraries.

MQPress: How did libraries contribute to your early career as a writer?

Carman: In a couple of ways. The first book that I wrote, *The Dark Hills Divide,* the first people to read it and kind of help me move it along were librarians in my own hometown. I lived in Walla Walla, Washington which is a small town. Not a huge library. But I spent a lot of time down there. Primarily just reading and a quiet place to study and write and hang out.

MQPress: What types of reading materials or books are in your personal book collection or library?

Carman: I visit a lot of schools. I've been to almost four hundred schools. Kids are always asking me, "What's your favorite book? What's your favorite book?" I don't actually read a lot of books that are for young readers. As far as fantasy books, because I write fantasy and science fiction, I don't even read a lot of those. My library is filled primarily with adult fiction or adult literature or a lot of classics. I like a lot of old classic novels. As far as fantasy I do have *Lord of the Rings*. I have several different versions of that series. I love that series. Mostly a lot of books written for adults.

MQPress: Besides libraries, what other resources do you use to research your writing?

Carman: I use the Internet[1] a lot. Online newspapers and archives. I interview a lot of people.

MQPress: What value do you believe libraries have to the general public?

Carman: The great thing about libraries is they're a great equalizer the same way public schools are equalizers. Any kid can walk into a library and get the books that they want. So that's what I love about libraries.

MQPress: How have you used libraries for your latest work?

Carman: I sort of got into a routine about a year and a half ago where I was reading a lot of old gothic novels. I got them from my library. *Turn of the Screw* is a book that I read and also *Frankenstein* when I was researching for this new novel. I just picked them up from the library.

♩ ♩ ♩ ♩ ♩ ♩ ♩ ♩ ♩ ♩ ♩ ♩ ♩ ♩ ♩

---

[1] The Internet is a gathering of computer networks that transmit data using standard Internet Protocol. Various academic, business, non-profit, and government computer networks carry services such as email, chat, file transfer, web pages, and the World Wide Web. The Internet is not the World Wide Web. While the Internet is a gathering of interconnected networks linked by hardware, the World Wide Web is a collection of interconnected resources, linked by hyperlinks and URLs. The World Wide Web is a service of the Internet.

Cooper Edens

Cooper Edens, both author and illustrator, won the Children's Critic Award for *The Starcleaner Reunion* which was also adapted as a ballet. With a long-standing relationship with Green Tiger Press, Edens' early works, *If You're Afraid of the Dark, Remember the Night Rainbow*, and *The Starcleaner Reunion* remained in publication for over three decades. He has also compiled several works such as *The Glorious Mother Goose* and *Beauty and the Beast.*

Interview at American Library Association Mid-Winter Meeting. Seattle, WA. 2007

MQPress: Please describe your earliest experience as a library user, visitor, patron, or customer.

Edens: As a twelve-year-old boy, or maybe even younger, I had an incredible desire to see how many beautiful birds there were where I didn't live. And so I remember going to the small library and was just overwhelmed by the variety of birds that I wouldn't otherwise have known about and the colors and the patterns. I think that inspired me to put a lot of birds in my stories. And I always knew the exact colors because the library helped me.

MQPress: How did libraries contribute to your early career as a writer?

Edens: Well, certainly in being authentic in things I wanted to illustrate. And also finding things that I didn't even know existed. So I would go often to browse to look for things that were out of my realm of existence like panda bears and things that obviously weren't where I lived which was in Seattle.

MQPress: What types of reading materials or books are in your personal book collection or library?

Edens: This is really special because I go to Europe a lot. I get lots of antique books. Their range of cost is usually somewhere between $100 and $200. Which seems incredibly fair for books that are a hundred years old. I'm always going to Europe and looking for books from 1900.

MQPress: Besides libraries what other resources do you use to research your writing?

Edens: I actually use walks on the beach. Just looking around in my neighborhoods. I talk to people a lot. Ask them what they want. Walking. Unusual, yeah.

MQPress: What value do you believe libraries have to the general public?

Edens: It increases the reality or the fantasy or the dreams of being alive. So whatever you can find in your own life, including t.v. and movies and everything is great. But you can always count on the libraries to tell you about the past and the future and what people enjoy. It just gives you more dimension.

MQPress: How have you used libraries for your latest work?

Edens: My latest work is actually *Sea Stories*. First I thought of every sea story there was from *Sinbad the Sailor* to *The Little Mermaid*. And so then I was able to go to different libraries and find illustrations for those that were hard to find, sometimes impossible to find. This quite literally was my garden. I picked flowers and vegetables and put them in my book. And that's *Sea Stories* and that's with Chronicle Books.

♩   ♩   ♩   ♩   ♩   ♩   ♩   ♩   ♩   ♩   ♩   ♩   ♩   ♩   ♩

Phil Foglio

McQueen Press

Winner of two Hugo Awards for his art, Phil Foglio wrote and illustrated a strip about role-playing games for *Dragon Magazine*. He adapted *Another Fine Myth* of *Myth Adventure* into a comic book and worked with DC Comics, Marvel Comics, and First Comics. Foglio contributed art to *Magic: the Gathering* by Wizards of the Coast. Co-founder of Palliard Press, he published *Buck Godot* and *XXXenophile*. As founder of Studio Foglio, he created *girl genius*.

Interview at American Library Association Mid-Winter Meeting. Seattle, WA. 2007

MQPress: Please describe your earliest experience as a library user, visitor, patron, or customer.

Foglio: Well, gosh! Libraries were always present in the schools I attended. So I always found them a fascinating place to pick up the latest books and basically fill in gaps in my reading. I read a lot of science fiction and fantasy. So much so that the teachers complained about it and the librarians had to cut me off.

MQPress: How did libraries contribute to your early career as a writer?

Foglio: They had interesting books on words and word usage and development and history. I found that I loved finding out what words meant. You know, the little strange little stories you have about words, the etymology and stuff. Basically, my vocabulary got to the point where I was really useless for anything else.

MQPress: What types of reading materials or books are in your personal book collection or library?

Foglio: A lot of science fiction. A lot of fantasy. A lot of reference materials. A lot of art books and visual reference because I'm also an artist. Let's see… We also have just sections on everything. Sections on gardening. Sections on how to build things. Sections on mythology and history. We've got a couple of encyclopedias. Pretty much, we've got a lot of everything.

MQPress: Besides libraries what other resources do you use to research your writing?

Foglio: These days, my Google[2] skills are unsurpassed. In fact, I google a lot more than I actually physically go to the library these days.

MQPress: What value do you believe libraries have to the general public?

Foglio: At their most basic level, they're a warm, friendly place to get in out of the rain and find something to read. And they're free so they appeal to the lowest common denominator in that respect and work their way up. I think almost anybody can find something interesting and diverting in a good library.

MQPress: How have you used libraries for your latest work?

Foglio: For my latest work? I occasionally need obscure visual reference material. And I always listen to music while I write so I raid the CD collections.

♩　　♩　　♩　　♩　　♩　　♩　　♩　　♩　　♩　　♩　　♩　　♩　　♩　　♩　　♩

---

[2] Google Inc. is an American public corporation, specializing in Internet search and online advertising, whose mission is to "organize the world's information and make it universally accessible and useful." Being the largest online search engine, Google receives several hundred million queries each day.

J.A. Jance

Mary Ann Halpin Studios

J.A. Jance, a former librarian, is the New York Times bestselling author of the Joanna Brady police procedurals (*Desert Heat, Skeleton Canyon, Exit Wounds*, etc), the J.P. Beaumont police procedurals (*Until Proven Guilty, Trial by Fury, Partner in Crime*, etc) and the Walker thrillers (*Hour of the Hunter, Kiss of the Bees*, and *Day of the Dead*) and books for children. *Long Time Gone*, brings back policeman J.P. Beaumont and a new cold case of Seattle murder.

Interview at Seattle Mystery Bookshop. Seattle, Washington. 2007

MQPress: Please describe your earliest experience as a library user, visitor, patron, or customer.

Jance: In Bisbee, Arizona, the elementary school library at Greenway school was open during the summers. We dragged our Radio Flyer wagon back and forth loaded with wagon loads of library books. That really impacted my love of reading as a child.

MQPress: How did libraries contribute to your early career as a writer?

Jance: For my first thriller, *Hour of the Hunter,* I turned in seventy inter-library loan[3] requests for materials on the Tohono O'otham[4] reservation west of Tucson. And those came back and brought me to Karavill

---

[3] Inter-library loan [see Glossary of Library Terms].

[4] The Tohono O'odham Nation is a Native American tribe of approximately 24,000 members whose traditional name translates to "People of the Desert." Formerly known as Papago or "tepary-bean eaters" by Spanish conquistadors, their land base consists of the main reservation, San Xavier District, San Lucy District and Florence Village – southwest Arizona and northwest Mexico. The Tohono O'odham are closely related to the Pima Tribe and thought to be descendants of prehistoric Hohokam Culture. Known for a strong tradition of language, culture, and artisanship, many O'odham work for Tohono O'odham Nation, the federal government, are ranchers, or work in nearby cities like Phoenix and Tucson.

Wright's books. The book, *Long Ago Told*, which contained many of the legends that would otherwise be lost on the reservation.

MQPress: What types of reading materials or books are in your personal book collection or library?

Jance: I have a lot of mysteries. I write mysteries because I've always loved mysteries. But I also have a good deal of poetry. C. Day Lewis was one of my favorite poets. I grew up listening to my father read the *Treasury of the Familiar*. So I have poetry. For Christmas, my daughter gave me *Where the Sidewalk Ends*.

MQPress: Besides libraries, what other resources do you use to research your writing?

Jance: I use libraries and the Internet. The Internet has become a real short cut to get stuff these days that would have been a lot harder to locate in years past. Just last week, I was looking up short-hand words for instant messaging[5] because I'm writing a book where instant messaging plays a part. I was able to find an instant message dictionary on the Internet.

MQPress: What value do you believe libraries have to the general public?

Jance: For me, growing up in Bisbee, Arizona where there were no bookstores, libraries were the alternative. I just don't foresee that libraries are ever going to go out of fashion.

MQPress: How have you used libraries for your latest work?

Jance: I'm trying to figure out what *is* my latest work. There's my latest work that's out now or my latest work that's coming out in July or the latest work I'm working on for next year. That's a question I really can't answer easily.

♩　♩　♩　♩　♩　♩　♩　♩　♩　♩　♩　♩　♩　♩

---

[5] Instant message is real-time communication between two or more people through typed text on computer. The typed text is transmitted by computer network by the Internet or sometimes, an intranet.

Sheryl McFarlane

McQueen Press

Writer, Sheryl McFarlane, travels extensively to share her work and experience as a children's author at various libraries, schools, and fairs. She has written many children's books including *A Pod of Orcas, Waiting for the Whales, Tide of Change, Eagle Dreams*, and *What's That Sound?* Her recent work, *The Smell of Paint* (Fitzhenry & Whiteside) is a novel about a family dealing with grief told from the viewpoint of a teenage girl with talent in track and field.

Interview at American Library Association Mid-Winter Meeting. Seattle, WA. 2007

MQPress: Please describe your earliest experience as a library user, visitor, patron, or customer.

McFarlane: My earliest visit was with a bookmobile[6] in a very small town in Arizona, a small mining town. The bookmobile arrived. I went and checked out a book. I was probably about eight.

MQPress: How did libraries contribute to your early career as a writer?

McFarlane: Libraries contributed immensely. I spent quite a bit of time at the library. I looked at every picture book I could. I then gathered a list of all the award-winning books and read those books. I also looked at all the catalogs that publishers had. I started reading book reviews in the journals. Very helpful. Of course, speaking to librarians who gave a lot of assistance.

MQPress: What types of reading materials or books are in your personal book collection or library?

McFarlane: In my personal collection it is probably about ninety percent children's books. A very high percentage of picture books because I *love* picture books. And then there's some reference books. And then a small number of adult novels. And a little bit of non-fiction.

MQPress: Besides libraries, what other resources do you use to research your writing?

---

[6] Bookmobile [see Glossary of Library Terms].

McFarlane: I use experts in the field quite extensively. They're really important and really helpful. Most of my books that relate to any natural history things, I usually send them off to someone to vet. Also, experts in whatever area I'm writing about. I tend to read in those areas. But I also like to talk to people to pick up mistakes that you make that you otherwise wouldn't have noticed.

MQPress: What value do you believe libraries have to the general public?

McFarlane: I think they are extremely important in educating the public about reading and books as well as teachers and parents. They also provide lots of opportunities for kids and adults to interact with books. And they're really, really important in terms of people who do not have English as a first language. So they're really involved in integrating and for networking in the community for people for whom literacy is an issue.

MQPress: How have you used libraries for your latest work?

McFarlane: For my latest work, I used libraries for some of the statistics that went into the book. I also used the journals and looked at previous stories and newspapers related to the topics I was writing about. I used the Internet cafes as well because I was on the road when I was doing some of this. That was another handy thing to have access to.

Anthony Ellis McGee

A native of Chicago, McGee has poetry featured in *The Coming of Dawn*. With a background in the insurance industry, he has also volunteered with Illinois Literacy Volunteers of America as a reading tutor. His debut novel, *Under the Same Roof* (Author House) addresses the family dynamic of siblings raised together who nevertheless approach life's many challenges differently. Currently, he is working on his next novel.

McQueen Press

Interview at the Health and Wellness/Reading Festival. Chicago, IL. 2007

MQPress: Please describe your earliest experience as a library user, visitor, patron, or customer.

McGee: My earliest experience with libraries was way before the Internet. I would go there to do research papers, to get information, look up periodicals. And different things… If I needed information that was the first place I knew to go. Libraries from the age of probably eight or nine, was where I would go to get information. Growing up on the Southside, I was at Carter G. Woodson Library[7] and other libraries as well.

MQPress: How did libraries contribute to your early career as a writer?

McGee: Just the whole aspect of being able to go to the library and get books. And reading just helped me to develop my imagination and to see things and just to take me places I couldn't go physically. But I could go in my mind or use my imagination.

MQPress: What types of reading materials or books are in your personal book collection or library?

McGee: In my personal collection is fiction. I'm a fiction writer so I definitely like to read contemporary African-American fiction by, say, Terry McMillan, E. Lynn Harris, Omar Tyree. People like that. Also, I

---

[7] Carter G. Woodson Regional Library is a two-story, 72,000 square feet building, with a staff of approximately sixty which serves south and southwest Chicago, but also attracts patrons from all parts of Chicago and its south suburbs. From www.chicagopubliclibrary.org

like biographies and autobiographies because those type of books give you a blueprint of what individuals have had to go through to become successful in life. Stories like *Succeeding Against the Odds* by John H. Johnson and other books that are positive and can give insight into a person's development.

MQPress: Besides libraries what other resources do you use to research your writing?

McGee: Definitely the Internet. The Internet is like having a library at your fingertips. So I'm always googling, looking up different things that may lead me to more facts that I'm trying to find.

MQPress: What value do you believe libraries have to the general public?

McGee: I think the value is tremendous. I think if children are able to go to a library at an early age and just discover the art and the fun of reading... I think if a person reads, there's nothing they can't accomplish. Because there's so much information and so much knowledge that can be gained just by picking up a book and finding something they're interested in. And sometimes, we're not even aware of some subjects might pique our interest until we pick up a book and start studying. One book that I encourage all children to read is a book by the name of *Gifted Hands* by Ben Carson and *Think Big*, - telling the story of Dr. Ben Carson, the neurosurgeon at Johns Hopkins, and how he became interested in medicine. So anytime that you can find books or magazines that can inspire you to go to another level, it's always beneficial to the individual.

MQPress: How have you used libraries for your latest work?

McGee: I use libraries oftentimes just to see what's on the shelves. To see what's out. To see what's hot. To see what types of materials are constantly in front of our faces. Libraries have so [many] different types of reading where you can find just about anything at anytime.

♩　♩　♩　♩　♩　♩　♩　♩　♩　♩　♩　♩　♩

Terry Moore

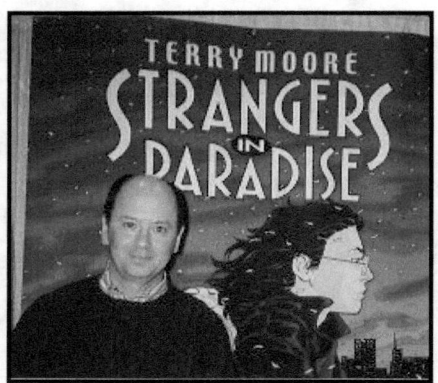

McQueen Press

Terry Moore published the first issue of *Strangers in Paradise* through Antarctic Press in 1993. He self-published through his own imprint, Abstract Studio, in 1994. *Strangers in Paradise* won the Eisner Award for Best Continuing Series in 1996. Moore launched Homage Comics with two partners in 1996 before returning to Abstract Studio to continue *Strangers in Paradise*, reprinted in seven languages. Soon to come are a novel and a syndicated comic strip.

Interview at American Library Association Mid-Winter Meeting. Seattle, WA. 2007

MQPress: Please describe your earliest experience as a library user, visitor, patron, or customer.

Moore: Like most readers, I used libraries at a very young age. I always was familiar with my local library. I used libraries extensively when I was researching my art career and my writing career. So they've always played a very important role in my life.

MQPress: How did libraries contribute to your early career as a writer?

Moore: I used the library as if it were my own expensive collection of books. Instead of me having the frame of mind where I had to own every book I like, I assume everything is in the library. I just let them hold my books for me. I go find the book I want there. That was my approach. When I was researching for both my art career I used the library looking for teaching materials, reference materials, historical education on the fields. Everything I looked for was there. Plus the people in the library were very helpful in saving me time so I didn't have to start from scratch. There were experts to guide me straight towards my needs.

MQPress: What types of reading materials or books are in your personal book collection or library?

Moore: My personal collection, I try to keep at a set number. I focus mostly on either my particular interest or on things that are very useful to me for my interests. I tend to read popular fiction, everything from thrillers to classics. But I also have a large selection of resource materials such as specialized books on anatomy or chemistry. Even a book on poisons if need it for my stories. I'm also very interested in the sciences and technology which helps me to develop junk science ideas for my stories. So I think I have a pretty broad selection of titles on my bookshelves.

MQPress: Besides libraries, what other resources do you use to research your writing?

Moore: Well, I use the Internet. There's a computer near the drawing table and if I have a question about what anything looks like, I can find it quickly on the Internet. I also tend spell-check myself or use the thesaurus functions on the computer. I also use Google Earth to look at street maps and layouts now and things like that. That's all very helpful to me. I guess the difference to me between the library and the Internet is the Internet is good for the quick answer. I don't have to leave my chair. The library is where I would expect to find all the books and printed material that I would ever expect to find in history. Hopefully, everything in history is in the library.

MQPress: What value do you believe libraries have to the general public?

Moore: I think that they're very valuable in terms of what has happened before you. But also, in looking at the material, an educated reader can tell what's going to come as well. [Libraries] educate you about the past, what can be what could be written. It's just not a building of history. It's also a building where tomorrow's writers can form ideas.

MQPress: How have you used libraries for your latest work?

Moore: Well, I've used them to do the research. I've used them to keep up with my peers. There are a lot of graphic novels[8] out now. I'm finding it easier and easier to find new graphic novels in the libraries. I like that because I really can't afford to go out and buy every graphic novel that's written. I'm using the library as my own extended personal bookshelf.

♩   ♩   ♩   ♩   ♩   ♩   ♩   ♩   ♩   ♩   ♩   ♩   ♩   ♩   ♩

---

[8] A graphic novel is a form of comic book, which contains artwork crucial to translating the storyline or plot to the reader. However, the storyline is longer and more complex sharing that similarity with traditional novels. Graphic novels generally have stronger binding than comic magazines.

John J. Nance

McQueen Press

John Nance's unique background includes journalism, law, military and commercial piloting. Not surprisingly, his writing crosses genres in seventeen major books from the technical non-fictions *Splash of Colors: the Self-Destruction of Braniff International, Blind Trust,* and *On Shaky Ground* to thriller fictions *The Last Hostage, Blackout,* and *Orbit.* Two of his novels, *Pandora's Clock* and *Medusa's Child* were adapted into television miniseries.

Interview at American Library Association Mid-Winter Meeting. Seattle, WA. 2007

MQPress: Please describe your earliest experience as a library user, visitor, patron, or customer.

Nance: Well, I'd have to go back a long time. Back into childhood. There are a lot of teachers that you remember. One of them, in probably fifth or sixth grade was Helen Morgan, I remember. We kind of laughed about her because she tended to read to the class. It was many years later that I realized how valuable that was. Not only her reading but also the fact that she got us familiar with going to the library as a kid when you're really intimidated by everything around you. When I started writing professionally, it was 1982, my airline, Braniff International, had collapsed. May 12, 1982, in fact. And I had an opportunity to start writing which meant I had to do a lot of research. The very first library I walked into was down in Los Angeles, UCLA's main library. From there, it was a matter of almost living in various libraries to get those first four books, which were all non-fiction, done. One about the collapse of Braniff. One about human factors in aviation and safety. One about earthquakes which took a huge amount of research. One about global warming and atmosphere. But my research, lately, has its beginning in each instance with the Internet, but it always leads back to the library for intensive research.

MQPress: How did libraries contribute to your early career as a writer?

Nance: As I said, the first four books out of eighteen were non-fiction. Fourteen fiction and the rest non-fiction. The first four would not have been possible without the help of libraries. All over the country, the fun part was wherever I was, I could always find a library. In some cases, doing the book on earthquakes in Alaska, that was my third one in 1988, some of the archives that were available that had not been put on public display were critical in being able to piece together something that happened in 1964 which was a mainstream event for the story.

MQPress: What types of reading materials or books are in your personal book collection or library?

Nance: I do actually have about a two-story bookshelf array down in my home and office in Tacoma. I've got some things that are really interesting to refer to. Every *National Geographic* since 1911. Even though you can get it summarized on DVDs, it's fun to be able to pull out the actual magazine. A lot of magazines, a lot of medical books from my wife's grandfather who was a country doctor, legal books. Various and sundry things over the years. It's strange how even with a thousand or more books your mind will keep them cataloged. Sometimes you don't know exactly where they are. We're not with the Dewey Decimal System[9] in that library. It's more like about what we remember doing last week. But you can still put your hands on something you hadn't thought about in six or seven years.

MQPress: Besides libraries what other resources do you use to research your writing?

Nance: There is no question that here in 2007, the Internet has become an incredible tool. It's a shadow of what it's going to be in ten or twenty years. Where the entirety of the knowledge of mankind is going to start becoming available at your finger tips with the ease of a search. It's what Google wants to do[10] and I think they're going to accomplish it. Even

---

[9] Melvil Louis Kossuth Dewey (1851-1931) was an American librarian, educator, and activist born in Adams Center, New York. While a student worker in the Amherst College library in 1876, Dewey originated the Decimal Classification System [see Glossary of Library Terms] named after him. He founded the first school for scientific training of librarians, the School of Library Economy in 1884. He was a crucial force in the founding of the American Library Association. He became the first editor of *Library Journal*. He pioneered the introduction of standardized supplies, equipment, and methods in librarianship. After experiencing concern regarding the co-education of women, he was appointed secretary of the Board of Regents, 1889-1990, and State Librarian of New York, 1889-1906, while at the New York State Library School in Albany (which became a unit of Columbia University in 1926).

[10] Google partnered with various publishers and universities to introduce a program, Fall 2004, called Google Book Search to help users search through the world's books

today, I can throw a question into that machine and get back a response that may not be definitive but it gets me on the right track. Where I would have had to spend four or five days in a library and just hope for luck to be able to snag the right things. I can do that in a microsecond now. The ability to bring to the human family a mass of knowledge in a way that at least can at least answer questions if not provide a standing repository of knowledge is changing the world. There's no question about it. And libraries are foremost in this as they begin to computerize not only what they've got on the stacks, but as the Library of Congress[11] is doing, more and more things are being put into actual online access. A hundred years from now there won't be anything in a library that isn't instantly available and accessible. But the role of the librarian and the role of the library will be even more important.

MQPress: What value do you believe libraries have to the general public?

Nance: Well, there's no question that even though it's a declining market for hardback and paperback books, people are reading less. They are listening to more audio. They have video, of course, in various forms has not really picked up on books yet outside the movies but that's going to pick up. I think the value to society is the same one that Andrew Carnegie[12] saw when he decided to put his money into a chain

---

and to help authors and publishers promote their books and expand their sales. When a user types in a search term, pointers to books that contain the search term are included in the results. Google's mission is to organize the world's information into a type of comprehensive electronic card catalog of the world's books by working with libraries. Google's program has been debated in terms of consistency to The Copyright Act. Google offers publishers and copyright holders the procedure to exclude their titles from Google Book Search. Condensed from Google's *The Facts About Google Book Search.*

[11] Library of Congress [see Glossary of Library Terms].

[12] Andrew Carnegie (1835-1919) was an American iron and steel industrialist born in Scotland. Carnegie felt that the man of wealth had a responsibility to society. Man must use his fortune to provide greater opportunities for everyone and to increase knowledge of self and the universe. Carnegie began building libraries starting with his native town of Dunfermline in 1882. He provided funds for a total of 2057 libraries throughout the English-speaking world – 1689 in the United States, 660 in Great Britain and Ireland, 125 in Canada – some say for the purpose of assimilating immigrants into mainstream society. Carnegie also felt that wealth for the benefit of society must not be free charity but instead used to support a community's responsibility for its own welfare. For each library, Carnegie provided funds for the building but only after the municipal government provided a site and passed an ordinance for the purchase of books and maintenance of the library through taxation. Carnegie established numerous trusts and foundations through which he gave back over $300,000,000 to society during his lifetime.

of libraries around the country which was a wonderful gift to the country. People need to understand the value of just reading. If we lose that, we are going to lose ourselves as a society. In the forefront of that is the peace and quiet and tranquility and the ability to think which is inherent to sitting in a library The instant gratification world that we're in now with everyone carrying ipods around, I've got one too, there are times when there's too much cacophony to think. You really do need the voice of the printed word coming through the page sitting in a quiet environment. If people lose that ability to walk into a library and think, 'My God, so much knowledge, so little time,' then we've lost something very profound.

MQPress: How have you used libraries for your latest work?

Nance: Well, pretty much for specific research. For instance, the book *Orbit* which came out a year ago, which is just about to come out in paperback, was set in space. I'm the aerospace analyst for ABC *World News* and *Good Morning, America*.[13] For space, it's so complex that I have to actually pull monographs off the shelf and look at more than the cursory stuff to make sure I get it right. I had to make several trips to the library. It was kind of fun because I hadn't done that for several books in several years.

◢ ◢ ◢ ◢ ◢ ◢ ◢ ◢ ◢ ◢ ◢ ◢ ◢ ◢

---

[13] John Nance is also described as Aviation Analyst for *ABC World News* and Aviation Editor for *Good Morning America* at the John Nance Productions website http://www.johnjnance.com/.

Matthew Olshan

McQueen Press

Educated at Harvard, Johns Hopkins, and Oxford universities, Olshan lists C.S. Lewis, Lewis Carroll, and Edward Lear as literary influences. *Finn: a novel* (Bancroft Press) updates Mark Twain's *The Adventures of Huckleberry Finn* highlighting the issues of immigration and class instead of slavery. *The Flown Sky* (Chacmool Press), described as "a novel of adventure, anagrams, and high literary nonsense" is based on a legend from Jewish mysticism.

Interview at American Library Association Summer Meeting. Washington, DC. 2007

MQPress: Please describe your earliest experience as a library user, visitor, patron, or customer.
Olshan: I guess it would be the library in elementary school in Washington – Sheridan School. Sitting in a kind of a pit with a helpful librarian offering me books to read.

MQPress: How did libraries contribute to your early career as a writer?
Olshan: By inspiring me to add a book to the groaning shelves at my home. By fueling my imagination. By shaping my literary sensibilities. So basically in every important way.

MQPress: What types of reading materials or books are in your personal book collection or library?
Olshan: I'm an eclectic reader. So I have certain categories of interest. I write fiction so I have a lot of fiction in the house. I also find strange books and sometimes use them for story ideas. I guess I have fiction that interests me and non-fiction that might lead to fiction. And then, other books just find their way into the house so they're there too.

MQPress: Besides libraries what other resources do you use to research your writing?

Olshan: Actually, these days, I use the Internet a lot more than the libraries. And I also find myself using Amazon.com's[14] used book sales area. I'll find something that I think will be useful and then for five dollars I can have it shipped to me directly. I can keep the book. Which for my writing is helpful. Sometimes I like to hang on to a book for a long time. Renewing a book would be sort of a hassle instead of owning a book and I have plenty of space.

MQPress: What value do you believe libraries have to the general public?

Olshan: I think they're irreplaceable. I think they're central to the idea of a civilized life and a country. I'm glad that Ben Franklin had the idea of establishing free lending libraries.[15] I think it's great. I think the dissemination of knowledge is crucial to humankind survivability. So aside from their social value and the community value, I think they have the key civilizing value too.

MQPress: How have you used libraries for your latest work?

Olshan: For my very latest work, I haven't used the library. I've been using the Internet. Well actually, libraries often have an information desk and I'll make use of that service. But I haven't had to go to a library to find a book in a long time. Because between Amazon.com and Ebay,[16] you can typically find a used version of whatever you're looking for, supplement that with online resources and personal interviews, and then

---

[14] Amazon.com, Inc. is an American e-commerce company based in Seattle, Washington. Founded in 1994 by Jeff Bezos, and launched in 1995, Amazon.com began as an online bookstore, although it has since diversified its products.

[15] Benjamin Franklin (1706-1790) was an American printer, publisher, author, diplomat, philosopher, inventor, and scientist. Apprenticed at the age of thirteen to his brother, James, he learned the printing trade and wrote anonymous articles for his brother's paper, *The New England Courant*. He organized a debate society in 1727 known as the "Junto" which later developed into the American Philosophical Society. He became owner of *The Pennsylvania Gazette* in 1729 and published *Poor Richard's Almanac* in 1732. He founded the first subscription library in North America in 1731 called The Library Company of Philadelphia which became the prototype for social libraries. Shareholders pooled their money to buy a collection of books, mostly from England, to which all stockholders had access. To raise funds, non-shareholders were eventually allowed access to the collection for a rental fee. In 1742, The Library Company of Philadelphia was chartered as the Philadelphia Library. In 1749, Franklin wrote *Proposals Relating to the Education of Youth* in Pennsylvania which led to the establishment of the Philadelphia Academy in 1751 which later became the University of Pennsylvania.

16 Ebay Inc. manages an auction network founded in 1995 that is used to buy and sell goods and services online. Although commerce occurs worldwide, the company is headquartered in the United States and includes other businesses.

you're all set. So my need for the library is dwindling. But my respect for libraries and the belief that they're crucial has not altered.

♩   ♩   ♩   ♩   ♩   ♩   ♩   ♩   ♩   ♩   ♩   ♩   ♩   ♩

David Ufer

David Ufer is a first-time children's author whose book, *The Giraffe Who Was Afraid of Heights* (Sylvan Dell Publishing) stars a giraffe, a hippopotamus, and a vervet monkey who face down a crocodile. A 2006 Book Sense Children's Pick modeled after *The Wizard of Oz*, *The Giraffe* takes place in the African savannah. Educators at the Houston Zoo verified the book for scientific accuracy. Ufer donates ten percent of the royalties to the worthy World Wildlife Fund.

Interview at American Library Association Mid-Winter Meeting. Seattle, WA. 2007

MQPress: Please describe your earliest experience as a library user, visitor, patron, or customer.

Ufer: Well, I guess I remember as a child going to a wonderful library in Burganfield, New Jersey. It was a two-story library. I thought that was the greatest thing in the world to have two floors worth of books to run around, through and check out. We always went there. I always checked out books and read them voraciously and couldn't wait to go back and get more.

MQPress: How did libraries contribute to your early career as a writer?

Ufer: Well, I'm new to the writing experience. I just always loved going to the libraries and reading books. It must have just ingrained in me that books were good things to have and enjoyable to read.

MQPress: What types of reading materials or books are in your personal book collection or library?

Ufer: I have lots of books on writing, how to write, how to edit. Dialogue. Lots of science fiction. Stephen King, Anne Rice books. Lots of cookbooks and magazines. General knowledge books.

MQPress: Besides libraries, what other resources do you use to research your writing?

Ufer: Definitely the Internet. The Internet is always a wonderful tool. Most libraries have Internet access[17] or their websites on the Internet. So you can do library research without actually having to go to the library.

MQPress: What value do you believe libraries have to the general public?

Ufer: In my experience, as a young child, it's very important to have access to materials that kids can learn from. Just to escape the everyday world into the fantasy world.

MQPress: How have you used libraries for your latest work?

Ufer: I use libraries to promote my book [*The Giraffe Who was Afraid of Heights*], mostly. I go to libraries and read to the kids that are at the libraries. All kinds of events at the library. Unfortunately, most of my research is done on the Internet. But I do go to libraries, mostly right now, for book events for my own book.

♩　♩　♩　♩　♩　♩　♩　♩　♩　♩　♩　♩　♩　♩　♩　♩

---

[17] Bill Gates (1955-) is an American business leader and software architect born in Seattle, Washington. As the largest shareholder of Microsoft, Gates is one of the world's richest men, a leading entrepreneur, and a dominant figure in the computing industry. Gates feels that even though PCs and technology can often be part of a solution for society's problems, those who are able should remember to put technology into service for humanity and that meeting human needs is the start of humanity. The mission of the Bill & Melinda Gates Foundation's Global Libraries Program is to ensure that everyone, regardless of age, race, gender, or income has access to the Internet and the new world of digital information. In U.S. and international libraries, there is continuous need for wire installation, hardware and software upgrades, Internet connections, technical support, technology training and instruction. Because of this, at the end of 2004, the Gates Foundation allocated approximately $9 million in financial assistance since it began the program in 2000. Similar to library philanthropist Andrew Carnegie, Gates also feels that it is important for the broader community to step up and participate in the cause in order to maintain access to public computing. For this reason, his foundation issues challenge grants whereby the foundation matches funds raised by a state at a 2-1 ratio. In addition, Gates seeks out partnerships with local governments, businesses, foundations, non-profits, and libraries.

Suzanne Williams

McQueen Press

Prior to writing children's books, Suzanne Williams was herself, a librarian for ten years. Lately, she has published the well-received "Princess Power" series - both well-illustrated and well-alliterated with such titles as, *The Perfectly Proper Prince*, *The Charmingly Clever Cousin*, and the *The Awfully Angry Ogre* with HarperCollins Publishers. Additional titles are the *Mysterious, Mournful Maiden*, *The Stubbornly Secretive Servant*, and *The Gigantic Genuine Genie*.

Interview at American Library Association Mid-Winter Meeting. Seattle, WA. 2007

MQPress: Please describe your earliest experience as a library user, visitor, patron, or customer.

Williams: I remember that my parents used to take me and my two sisters and brother to the library every couple of weeks when I grew up in Eugene, Oregon. I remember going to Eugene Public Library and going through the children's section and that feeling of warmth you get walking into a library. One book, I guess, that sticks in my mind that I remember checking out is *Strawberry Girl*. I don't know why that one in particular. I always remember feeling comfortable in libraries. I guess that's it. And just liking to be there amongst all those books.

MQPress: How did libraries contribute to your early career as a writer?

Williams: I don't know many writers who don't love to read. Because, if you do love to read, obviously, you're going to be a big library user. So, I guess, in that way, like most writers, libraries contributed because I love to read. And I read a lot. In fact, libraries contributed in more than one way because when I grew up, I became an elementary school librarian and came into writing for children because of being a librarian first.

MQPress: What types of reading materials or books are in your personal book collection or library?

Williams: Because as a writer, I like to look back at books that are my favorites when I'm writing myself, I keep a small collection of children's books on my bookshelves. Ones that I like to read over and over again.

I also keep a certain amount of non-fiction books on topics that are helpful to me personally like books on finance or books on writing, of course. I've got a whole shelf full of books on writing. Books on health. That kind of thing.

MQPress: Besides libraries, what other resources do you use to research your writing?

Williams: I write all fiction so the kind of research I do is a little different probably from non-fiction writers. I do sometimes have to look up things I need in a book. Like, let's say, I need to know rules for playing volleyball or something like that. The Internet is a big help for that kind of thing.

MQPress: What value do you believe libraries have to the general public?

Williams: We all pay taxes for a number of things. I think libraries are the one I'm most glad to see my taxes go for. I use my public library - the one that's closest to my home probably two or three times a week. I get more benefit from that than anything else that belongs to the general public. I like going there just to sit and read magazines and browse. I can order things online these days which is even more wonderful and go there to pick them up. I guess, like I just said, out of just any institution, libraries and of course schools are the two most benefit to the general population.

MQPress: How have you used libraries for your very latest work?

Williams: Oh wow. I'm writing about flower fairies right now. How have I used libraries for that? Well, I have checked out, of course, other series by other authors that are writing about flower fairies. Just to see whether mine is different enough from what they're doing. And to see what kinds of things they write about. I guess that way it's influenced what I do. I can't say that they have any way for that particular group of books.

♩   ♩   ♩   ♩   ♩   ♩   ♩   ♩   ♩   ♩   ♩   ♩   ♩   ♩

Chapter 3

Poets
&
Lyricists

Poem – Imaginative expression that is essentially metrical or written according to stanzaic forms. As a literary form, poetry is generally synonymous with verse and is contrasted to the conventional prose of exposition, narrative, or argument. Literature that is singular for the affecting sound or imagery of its language.

Lyric – Short poem that conveys intense personal emotion or thought. Principally a poem that is sung.

Rita Dove

Fred Viebahn

Commonwealth Professor of English at the University of Virginia, Rita Dove, holds the Pulitzer Prize, National Book Award, Carl Sandburg Award, Heinz Award, and National Humanities Medal. She was appointed Poet Laureate of the United States ('93-'95) and Virginia ('04-'06). Known for *Thomas and Beulah*, *Through the Ivory Gate*, *On the Bus with Rosa Parks*, and *American Smooth*, she provides lyrics for classic sound recordings.

Maple Valley Branch Library, 1967

For a fifteen-year-old there was plenty
to do: Browse the magazines,
slip into the Adult Section to see
what vast *tristesse* was born of rush-hour traffic,
décolletés, and the plague of too much money.
There was so much to discover--how to
lay out a road, the language of flowers,
and the place of women in the tribe of Moost.
There were equations elegant as a French twist,
fractal geometry's unwinding maple leaf;

I could follow, step-by-step, the slow disclosure
of a pineapple Jell-O mold--or take
the path of Harold's purple crayon through
the bedroom window and onto a lavender
spill of stars. Oh, I could walk any aisle
and smell wisdom, put a hand out to touch
the rough curve of bound leather,
the harsh parchment of dreams.

As for the improbable librarian
with her salt and paprika upsweep,
her British accent and sweater clip
(mom of a kid I knew from school)--
I'd go up to her desk and ask for help
on bareback rodeo or binary codes,
phonics, Gestalt theory,
lead poisoning in the Late Roman Empire,
the play of light in Dutch Renaissance painting;
I would claim to be researching
pre-Columbian pottery or Chinese foot-binding,

but all I wanted to know was:
Tell me what you've read that keeps
that half smile afloat
above the collar of your impeccable blouse.

So I read *Gone with the Wind* because
it was big, and haiku because they were small.
I studied history for its rhapsody of dates,
lingered over Cubist art for the way
it showed all sides of a guitar at once.
All the time in the world was there, and sometimes
all the world on a single page.
As much as I could hold
on my plastic card's imprint I took,

greedily: six books, six volumes of bliss,
the stuff we humans are made of:
words and sighs and silence,
ink and whips, Brahma and cosine,
corsets and poetry and blood sugar levels--
I carried it home, five blocks of aluminum siding
and the old garage where, on its boarded-up doors,
someone had scrawled:

I CAN EAT AN ELEPHANT
IF I TAKE SMALL BITES.

Yes, I said, to no one in particular: *That's*
what I'm gonna do!

Dave Gegic

McQueen Press

Gegic has been a bookstore owner in the Wicker Park area of Chicago. Currently, he is publisher and editor-in-chief of Puddin' Head Press, a specialty house, found online, that publishes and distributes books in various genres including biography, computer, criticism, education, mythology, and photography. He is active in the poetry community and has arranged poetry readings at various Chicago venues such as *Estelle's*.

Interview at Poetry Fest. Harold Washington Library. Chicago, IL. 2007

MQPress: Please describe your earliest experience as a library user, visitor, patron, or customer.
Gegic: When I was a little kid, I used to go to the library. There's a book I loved called *Pets from the Pond* by [M.W.] Buck. I used to go there and take this book out continuously because it was about keeping frogs and turtles and stuff in your house and stuff. I remember going there and taking it out so often that my parents bought me my own copy. Because I was interested in science and biology and stuff like that I was going to the library and having my mother go and get adult books out for me on biology and chemistry and stuff. Eventually, they gave me special permission in the library to go and get adult books out from the adult section. I could only go in the science and non-fiction section. But I was a ten-year-old kid in the adult section of the library and it was pretty neat.

MQPress: How did libraries contribute to your early career as a writer?
Gegic: I'm also a chemist. I do a little bit of technical writing for metal finishing journals and things of that sort. Those early experiences in the library made me a better chemist. It also introduced me to books I normally wouldn't have read. For example, Pearl Buck is somebody who wrote mostly fiction about China and stuff like that and introduced me to that. And then there was the poetry section. I was writing something. I wasn't sure what it was called at the time. But I was a pretty voracious

reader. Some of the stuff I was reading was poetry. And I was actually writing poetry even though I didn't know it at the time.

MQPress: What types of reading materials or books are in your personal book collection or library?

Gegic: Personally, I own about fifteen thousand books. Maybe even a little bit more than that. I also used to own a bookstore. I kept a lot of books from when I owned the bookstore. So, I have about fifteen or sixteen thousand books. Some of those are kind of slated to be sold. But they're also sloshed back and forth between my personal book collection and books that I sell. Some books that I would like to sell, I haven't been able to and I keep them in my own personal collection. So I have a big collection of books on writing. I got a huge science fiction collection and a huge poetry collection. Thousands and thousands of books.

MQPress: Besides libraries what other resources do you use to research your writing?

Gegic: Talking to people. I've been using the Internet more and more. Also old books that I own myself I use for research. Magazines. I use magazines for research a lot. One thing that I use that I get extensively from the library are books-on-tape. I drive probably an hour and a half to two hours everyday. I usually have a book-on-tape in there. I just finished a book-on-tape of Colin Powell's biography. Right now, I'm listening to a tape of *Devices and Desires* by P.D. James. I'm listening to that currently as a book-on-tape. I probably go through four or five books-on-tape per month from the library. I would buy those myself. I could never afford to do it. I would go broke. So I'm saving a hundred dollars per month by going to the library and getting those.

MQPress: What value do you believe libraries have to the general public?

Gegic: I used to run Reading for Teens at the Oak Park Library. The most teens we ever got there was a hundred and thirty. On a Friday night, there were kids that came to the library because they thought it was cooler to go to the poetry reading than to hang out at the park across the street and drink and do drugs. We ran that for like eight years and would get twenty to sixty kids, typically, on a Friday night. And that was a safe place for them to hang out. So it was important for the teens. I think the libraries are a way under-used resource. It took me years before I actually went and got a library card. I had one when I was a kid. But there was a fifteen year gap that I didn't have a library card. Why go to the library when I can buy the book? It's definitely an underused resource. There's actually a couple of projects I started… that I would to the library to get any kind information I could on a topic. I've been able to figure out how to do certain things just by resources from the library.

MQPress: How have you used libraries for your latest work?

Gegic: I am right now working on a couple more scientific kind of projects. I'm working on a book about water. I'm working on a science fiction story about future times. I've been using the Internet more than I've been using the library. I have used the library for different projects when I needed to know about like the history of the atom and things like that. But lately, I haven't been using the library very much.

Quraysh Ali Lansana

McQueen Press

Lansana is the Director of the Gwendolyn Brooks Center and Assistant Professor of English and Creative Writing at Chicago State University and former faculty of Julliard's Drama School. Co-editor of *Roll Call* and editor *of African American Literature Reader*, Lansana has also served on Third World Press, *Black Issues Book Review*, and Tia Chucha Press editorial boards. His works include *They Shall Run–Harriet Tubman Poems*, and *southside rain*.

Telephone interview at Chicago State University. Chicago, IL. 2007

MQPress: Please describe your earliest experience as a library user, visitor, patron, or customer.
Lansana: When I was in Head Start. I think it was after school with a really great librarian. A really wonderful librarian named Ms. Christopher, the mother of one of my older sister's best friends. I actually spent a great deal of time in libraries even before kindergarten. So my relationship with books started probably when I was about three or four actually.

MQPress: How did libraries contribute to your early career as a writer?
Lansana: I think because I've always been fascinated with language libraries have always been, since preschool, one of my favorite places to be. As an adult and as a published author, I was always sort of stunned that there seemed to be a real disconnect between writers and libraries in terms of writers reading and presenting in libraries. In the 80s and 90s I've seen that come about in a major way. So for me, libraries have always represented a place to get lost in ideas and history and knowledge... and a center for research. Particularly with my most recent folio book,[18] *They Shall Run-Harriet Tubman Poems* which are historically

---

[18] In bookbinding, a folio is a sheet of paper, parchment, or other material folded in half to make two leaves in a codex. Used mainly for manuscripts, the pages are often traditionally physically marked with numbers, and referred to, by folio number, with

based poems, I spent a lot of time in libraries particularly at the Schomburg Center[19] for black culture and research in New York. Researching primary documents and other books on the Underground Railroad[20] and what I could find on Harriet Tubman because she did not leave a paper trail herself. She never learned to read or write. The libraries always played an important role in my work largely because my work is rooted contextually in Black American and African diasporic politic culture and ideas. So I have always sought knowledge and inspiration from books in the library. Libraries have always have been that great resource for those ideas.

MQPress: What types of reading materials or books are in your personal book collection or library?

Lansana: That varies. Certainly, there are probably hundreds if not thousands of poetry books. Fiction. Non-fiction. Collections on writing. Poetry and craft. Chap books[21] by authors locally and nationally who have yet to publish their first book. I've worked as an editor in educational publishing for three major textbook publishers so textbooks are real dear to me. Textbooks as well, particularly in reading and language arts for k-12 students. Magazines and journals, lots of journals. Creative writing magazines. What else can I tell you? I'm a real history buff. So many, many books on Black history and African history and ideas. Books from other cultures or on other cultures that contain writings from other folks of color around the globe. A lot of very good poetry. A very diverse collection of poetry from folks from around the world.

MQPress: Besides libraries what other resources do you use to research your writing?

"recto" for the first side and "verso" for the second. Folio also refers to a book printed on folio pages.

[19] A division of New York Public Library, The Schomburg Center for Research in Black Culture collects, preserves, and provides access to resources documenting the history of persons of African descent throughout the world. Recognized on a national and international level, the research center also sponsors programs and events to illuminate and illustrate Black history and culture.

[20] The Underground Railroad was a secret network of routes (rails) and safe houses (stations) that African slaves in the United States used to escape to free states in the north and west, Canada, or Mexico, either alone or with the aid of abolitionists (conductors). Between 1810 and 1860, an estimated 100,000 people escaped enslavement via the Underground Railroad. Levi Coffin, a Quaker, John Brown, an abolitionist, and Harriet Tubman, an escaped slave, were the most active conductors.

[21] A chap book is a small book or pamphlet of popular tales, ballads, or poems.

Lansana: The Internet. And whenever possible to actually go to the source. Go to the place from which the ideas emanate. For example, when I was working on the Harriet Tubman book, I went to her home which is now a museum and did some work in that area [Auburn, NY]. I went to her gravesite. I spent some time on some Underground Railroad routes for the immediate experience. So whenever possible to go to the actual place or site where the research is rooted and experience it on your own. Sort of an immediate interpretation of the knowledge from the research. Very experiential sort of thing. Interviews. Other sources from either historians or books that I can access on whatever subject matter I'm researching.

MQPress: What value do you believe libraries have to the general public?

Lansana: Libraries are very under-utilized temples of knowledge and power and empowerment in our communities. It would be a wonderful thing if more and more folks thought that way and accessed a library card so they could access the knowledge therein access the power that is oftentimes free. I think libraries are very, very important particularly in the United States when funding for arts – music and other sorts of arts and cultural activities - in public schools have been removed. Libraries provide a valuable resource for students (adult learners as well as k-12 learners) to dream, to think, to access possibilities beyond their block, their neighborhoods. I think they are extremely, extremely important for the population. It is my hope and my dream for more young people and others to access them. One of my favorite programs in the city is the Neighborhood Writing Alliance where the organization presents free workshops for anyone interested in writing. Sort of a street corner philosopher sort of situation. Or anyone interested writing can come and write their truths, write their lives, write their stories, write about whatever they want. They have a journal called the *Journal of Ordinary Thought* where folks can publish. Their writings are published, which is source of real empowerment in my mind. Where folks who unlike me who didn't go to graduate school in creative writing but have something to say. And everyone does. I think that's a great example of how libraries can help empower folks who seek it and I wish more folks would.

MQPress: How have you used libraries for your latest work?

Lansana: The manuscript in progress? As I mentioned, for the Tubman book I spent a lot of time at the Schomburg, the Bobst Library[22] at

---

[22] Elmer Holmes Bobst Library is the main library of New York University. Bobst is one of the largest academic libraries in the United States with over three million

NYU and other places. For the work that I have in progress, which is largely autobiographical in terms of my own poetry, I will be spending more time in libraries researching, in particular, American Indian history and Black history in my birth state of Oklahoma. Because that factors prominently in the next book of poetry. I'm also in the process of editing several anthologies so it's been necessary to access literature and resource information on some of the writers who are being featured in some of these books. So I will be spending more and more time, particularly this summer, in any number of libraries. Particularly the Woodson and the Harsh Collection[23] doing some research for both my own manuscript of poetry in progress and these anthologies as well.

⌐ ⌐ ⌐ ⌐ ⌐ ⌐ ⌐ ⌐ ⌐ ⌐ ⌐ ⌐ ⌐ ⌐ ⌐

---

volumes, twenty thousand journals, and over three million microforms. Approximately one million books circulate daily and about 6500 people visit daily. From Wikipedia.

[23] The Vivian Harsh Collection situated within Woodson Regional Library in Chicago, holds the largest African American history and literature collection in the Midwest. Their collections include: 70,000 books (many rare), 500 periodical titles (current and retrospective) 75 microfilm research collections (totaling over 5000 reels), and significant primary source materials including manuscripts. From www.chicagopubliclibrary.org

Raúl Niño

McQueen Press

Chicagoan, Niño, won the Sister Cities Award in 1992 and traveled to Mexico City on a reading tour. Gwendolyn Brooks presented him the Significant Illinois Writers Award in 1993. His work appeared in *Power Lines* (Tia Chucha Press) and *New Chicano/Chicana Writers* (University of Arizona Press). His first poetry collection, *Breathing Light* (March Abrazo), was published in 1991. The latest is *Book of Mornings* (March Abrazo). Soon to come is *Rough Sutra.*

Interview at Poetry Fest. Harold Washington Library. Chicago, IL. 2007

MQPress: Please describe your earliest experience as a library user, visitor, patron, or customer.

Niño: Well that all started when I was a child in grade school. I practically lived in the school library. I spent all my time in the library other than being in the playground and being in the classroom. The English language, for me, was my second language. It took me a while to master it. The libraries helped me do that. I spent my time in the library looking at books, looking at pictures. And that was basically it. That's how I started.

MQPress: How did libraries contribute to your early career as a writer?

Niño: By seeing that people actually had careers as writers. By seeing their books and seeing the photographs and the covers of the books. Holding the books in my hand and realizing that this was something you could do for a living sometimes.

MQPress: What types of reading materials or books are in your personal book collection or library?

Niño: In my library at home I have a lot of books of poetry. I have books on nature, exploration, things like that. And reference books.

MQPress: Besides libraries what other resources do you use to research your writing?

Niño: Libraries are pretty much it except I do use the Internet. I make my living working in a library. I catalog books.[24] I work at a university research library. So I'm in libraries every day of my life pretty much.

MQPress: What value do you believe libraries have to the general public?

Niño: Oh my God. That's a pretty wide question. They are the core to our culture. They are the beating heart. Libraries and library systems in this country are beating heart of our U.S., American culture. They are indispensable.

MQPress: How have you used libraries for your latest work?

Niño: For my latest work, probably not so much. My latest work was written over ten years ago. We just recently got around to publishing it. It's a small chap book called *A Book of Mornings*. It's by March Abrazo Press and it just came out. Libraries didn't help the book directly. But the fact that I am in libraries everyday of my life is going to go into whatever I do work on.

♩　♩　♩　♩　♩　♩　♩　♩　♩　♩　♩　♩　♩

---

[24] Cataloger [see Glossary of Library Terms].

Sterling D. Plumpp

Plumpp has been Associate Professor at the University of Illinois, Chicago. He serves as editor for Third World Press and the Institute for Positive Education. An early work, *Clinton*, won the Illinois Arts Council Award for Poetry. He also holds the Carl Sandburg Literary Award for Poetry. Other works include *Black Rituals, The Mojo Hands Call, I Must Go, Somehow We Survive: An Anthology of South African Writing* and *Velvet BeBop Kente Cloth.*

McQueen Press

Interview at Poetry Fest. Harold Washington Library. Chicago, IL. 2007

MQPress: Please describe your earliest experience as a library user, visitor, patron, or customer.

Plumpp: Very early, in school, I found that the library was really the only value of school. In high school, I did not discover literature and technology. It was sometime later that I discovered James Baldwin. And in discovering James Baldwin, I discovered that my life could be literature.

MQPress: How did libraries contribute to your early career as a writer?

Plumpp: It forced me to leave the university. My early career as a writer had me literally leaving college and embarking on this arduous task of trying to find the meaning of life in the words of writers. So I would actually try to read a book a day.

MQPress: What types of reading materials or books are in your personal book collection or library?

Plumpp: I was fortunate to be a friend of a writer, Leon Forrest, who wrote *(unintelligible) Divine Days*. There's everything in my library from *(unintelligible)* stories to great poets like [Federico García] Lorca. Outstanding fiction writers like [William] Faulkner. And of course, Toni Morrison and Alice Walker.

MQPress: Besides libraries what other resources do you use to research your writing?

Plumpp: Well music probably has had and has a greater influence on me than libraries because I connect myself back to the land of my origins through music. Because it lives and continues to grow. Blues, today I suppose, is hip hop[25] and rap.[26] I'm angered at the hip hop and rap artists because none of them play instruments. Lyrically, they are in the next century, but they don't play instruments. I hear them. And film. I have always been moved by the most imaginative filmmakers. Probably from Spike Lee to Sam Peckinpah - *The Wild Bunch*. But the imaginative world of film, particularly black and white, affects my imagination. Film. The study of people. I was in South Africa twice. It indelibly shaped how I view the world. In South Africa, you have Nelson Mandela[27] who was in prison for twenty years. I went to his office. I edited a book *Somehow We Survive* and I dedicated it to him. Much later, he sent an autographed photograph of himself. The South African experience... people should know why those people died to get independence.

MQPress: What value do you believe libraries have to the general public?

Plumpp: I think now with the Internet, you have access to computers. It's how people define and redefine themselves daily. I think that the library is the essence of democracy. I think that if you close the libraries, it's like denying you the right to vote. It's like taking away your name. It's the tool that allows you to go hear people speak. But more importantly, it's the space that you own.

MQPress: How have you used libraries for your latest work?

Plumpp: My latest work, *Velvet BeBop Kente Cloth*. There's a thing called, "the book." Before, I read a lot of these poems in libraries. Sometimes with musicians over the last twenty years before I knew that I had a book. See I was reading and talking about, like today, things like that. The gathering... the creation of the space that became the audience of

---

[25] Hip hop is a cultural movement that encompasses music (rap), dance (breakdance), art (graffiti), and vocal expression (DJs and MCs). Hip hop developed in New York City starting in the 1970s, predominantly by African Americans and Latinos.

[26] Rap or rapping, also known as emceeing (MCing) is the rhythmic delivery of rhymes and is one of the central elements of hip hop music and culture. Raps are delivered either over a musical beat or without accompaniment. Derived from the griots (storytellers) of West Africa, Caribbean-style toasting, and American blues and jazz, rap is a meld of speech, prose, poetry, and song.

[27] Nelson Rolihlahla Mandela (1918-) is the former President of South Africa, and the first to be elected in fully representative democratic elections. Before his presidency, Mandela was an anti-apartheid activist and leader of the African National Congress. He spent twenty-seven years in prison for his struggle against apartheid.

the dialogue with other writers as I did today. Sometimes I get ideas for how to proceed with the book. I was forced to get someone to publish the book, but the library was the space where I dialogue. But fortunately, I was a teacher all those years and used the classroom... used the students as guinea pigs for my ideas. This book would not have been possible if I had not read a number of these poems at libraries. I see the Cultural Center as the library. It's Harold Washington now but when it was over there from the 1970s to the 1990s I was reading my poems there (at the Cultural Center) and meeting other writers. The Chicago Library was at Washington and Randolph. They moved [the library] here. There's a performance space, now they call it the Cultural Center. In other words, you get a cross-fertilization of ideas because you meet other people from different nationalities. I think that the library is the space. Books teach the writer to write. If I had not been a professor, I would need this library for its books. Now I just go upstairs and buy books. The relationship that I have with the people that I meet in libraries when I read and... I listen to what the poets say. The things that I can use I use.

♩　♩　♩　♩　♩　♩　♩　♩　♩　♩　♩　♩　♩　♩

Louis Reyes Rivera

Jenny Lau

Rivera taught Pan African, Caribbean, Puerto Rican, and African American history and literature at SUNY-Stonybrook, Hunter College, Pratt Institute, College of New Rochelle, etc. Poet, essayist, editor, and activist he holds the Special Congressional Recognition Award and works with jazz bands like Ahmed Abdullah's Diaspora, Sun Ra All-Star Project, and Jazzoets. Works include *Who Pays the Cost?*, *Yo!*, and *Bum Rush the Page: A Def Poetry Jam.*

Telephone interview at WBAI. New York City, NY. 2007

MQPress: Please describe your earliest experience as a library user, visitor, patron, or customer.

Rivera: I was about seven or eight years old. We used to have these huge library trucks. They were like neighborhood libraries. Portable. Or mobile. Mobile libraries.[28] They would park in various neighborhoods. Children would be encouraged to come on in, browse the shelves and read. We could borrow the books. Of course, that meant taking out my very first library card. How I learned to use the library to my benefit? I was eleven-years-old and I had seen this movie that had just come out. This was 1956. It was called *Chief Crazy Horse* with Victor Mature. I was totally fascinated by the fact that this was the first movie that I had seen where Native Americans actually defeated the white soldiers. The cavalry was always coming to somebody's rescue and wiping out the Indians. I was so taken by the storyline, when I went to school, we had a library hour every week. We were expected to spend ninety minutes in the library in my elementary school. You could do anything you wanted. So as soon as I got back to school, I asked the librarian how I could find out more about this person. And that's how I was introduced to all these various encyclopedias. So I started looking up Crazy Horse and then I found there were other people connected to him. And ended up getting a solid picture via various encyclopedia entries on that period and what those people were about. And it wasn't just Crazy Horse, there were a

---

[28] Bookmobile [see Glossary of Library Terms].

number of others involved in all of that. And that fascinated me. When I got into high school, the same thing happened with a movie called *Lawrence of Arabia* with Peter O'Toole. I was so taken with that storyline, that I immediately went and started researching [T.E. Lawrence] in various encyclopedias. I found out he'd written two books. One was called *Seven Pillars of Wisdom* and the other called [*Revolt in the Desert*] regarding the Arab Revolt. This was circa 1916, World War I. So I went and got his books and started reading what he'd written. I found out he wasn't the only British or French person attempting to organize Arab nomads.

MQPress: How did libraries contribute to your early career as a writer?

Rivera: I got to understand that anything I wanted to write about I needed to cross-reference and study the particulars involved. When I decided that writing was what I wanted to do, that was at fifteen, I understood that there was a lot about writing I didn't know. That was alright with me. I promised myself from then on, I would take the time to learn all there was to know about writing. I did that by reading. The library and the bookstore and the streets and the bars – the saloons, the taverns – they became my curriculum, if you will. They became the hotbed of my understanding developing writing. So the library was a very useful place for me that. Any book that I couldn't own, I could always borrow. I was reading everything. I read the German philosophers.[29] The French[30] and Russian novelists.[31] The American transcendentalists.[32] The British poets.[33] The Irish dramatists.[34] I spent

---

[29] German philosophy is either (1) philosophy in the German language or (2) philosophy by Germans such as Leibniz, Kant, Hegel, Marx, Schopenhauer, Nietzsche, Weber, Martin Heidegger, and Ludwig Wittgenstein.

[30] French literature refers to (1) the literature of France or its émigrés, and to (2) the French-language literature of several independent nations once colonies or still colonies of France. Alexander Dumas, Marcel Proust, Jean-Jacques Rousseau, and Victor Hugo are important French writers.

[31] Russian literature refers to (1) the literature of Russia or its émigrés, and to (2) the Russian-language literature of several independent nations formerly part Russia or the Soviet Union. Leo Tolstoy, Fyodor Dostoevsky, Vladimir Nabokov, Isaac Babel, Maxim Gorky, and Mikhail Bulgakov are leading Russian novelists.

[32] Transcendentalism emerged in early to mid-nineteenth century literature, religion, culture, and philosophy of New England (northeastern United States). Transcendentalism began as a protest against traditional culture and society, particularly, intellectualism at Harvard and the doctrine of the Unitarian church taught at Harvard Divinity School. A core belief was that the ideal spiritual state 'transcends' the physical and empirical states and that the ideal state is realized through an

nine years hunting all that down. Somewhere between the library and the bookstore would be my refuge, if you will.

MQPress: What types of reading materials or books are in your personal book collection or library?

Rivera: In my personal book collection I have a very extensive, you might say, eclectic area. I have lots of history books and sociology books that are basically European. I have a lot of Asian philosophy books. I have quite an extensive collection of Native American history and papers. I have a fascination for the Caribbean. I have an extensive collection on Caribbean history and literature and African history and literature.

MQPress: Besides libraries what other resources do you use to research your writing?

Rivera: I collect books. I've lost a good number of them. After I finished my bachelor's I hawked bookstores whenever I could looking for those materials that I didn't have. What the library does for me is let me see what it is and oftentimes, I want my own copy so I would return that to the library and then go hunt down a copy for myself. That was particularly throughout the 1970s and the 1980s. By 1986, I was noted for incorporating a lot of what I read into my poetry. Colleges began to offer me teaching positions because of the way I would weld what I was reading with what I was writing.

MQPress: What value do you believe libraries have to the general public?

Rivera: The value is inestimable. It allows the kind of access that you need in order to feed your brain cells in the same manner that you feed your stomach. I never understand how people can eat three sometimes four times per day and not want to read three or four times per day. Your thinking requires as much feeding as your body does.

MQPress: How have you used libraries for your latest work?

Rivera: Oh, that's interesting. My latest work is an epic poem that I've been working on for five years called *The Jazz in Jail*. *The Jazz in Jail* is a slightly historical work so that would necessitate that I keep working with books in my own library as well as in the public library. It required

---

individual's intuition, rather than established doctrines. Prominent Transcendentalists included Ralph Waldo Emerson and Henry David Thoreau.

[33] Some well-known British poets are William Shakespeare, Geoffrey Chaucer, John Milton, Samuel Johnson, John Keats, Alfred, Lord Tennyson, Robert Browning, and Elizabeth Barrett Browning.

[34] Some famous Irish playwrights include William Congreve, George Bernard Shaw, Oscar Wilde, and Samuel Beckett.

me to do a lot of research into music, musical trends, the personnel who developed or are noted for having developed various forms of jazz[35] throughout the years. One book, *Scattered Scripture,* was an attempt at me translating history into poetry so that each poem is reflective of a particular historical period or incident. The research I had to do required me to get to the library for various books that I didn't have. *Scattered Scripture* won an award back in 1996 when it was published. The Latin American Writers Institute cited the book as the best volume of poetry for 1996.

♩ ♩ ♩ ♩ ♩ ♩ ♩ ♩ ♩ ♩ ♩ ♩ ♩ ♩ ♩

---

[35] Jazz is an American music form that developed in New Orleans, Louisiana during the turn of the 20th century. Jazz uses improvisation, blue notes, swing, call and response, and syncopation. The roots of jazz combine West African music traditions such as spirituals, blues and ragtime as well as Western music traditions such as European military band style.

Marc Kelly Smith

Michael Acerra

Unveiling "poetry slam" at Chicago's Green Mill Tavern in 1987, Smith also performed at the Smithsonian Institute and was featured on *60 Minutes* and CNN. *Crowdpleaser*, his first book, was credited by *Chicago Sun Times* and *Chicago Tribune*. *Aloud! Voices from the Nuyorican Poets Café* and *The Outlaw Bible of American Poetry* feature his work. He wrote and produced plays *Flea Market: A Night of Monologues* and *A House Party for Henry*.

Interview at Uptown Poetry Slam. The Green Mill. Chicago, IL. 2007

MQPress: Please describe your earliest experience as a library user, visitor, patron, or customer.

Smith: In Chicago, the Cultural Center used to be the library. You know, the big building, but it wasn't set up very well to hunt things down. It was a gloomy place to go to. I wasn't a very good student. But in high school, I found a love of literature researching Mark Twain. I did it downtown at the Chicago Public Library. It was gloomy, but I found a lot of work by Mark Twain and actually read it. I got a good grade on it. It was kind of a spark for writing. Because I didn't know I wanted to write. But I started writing letters to a friend who went off to college in Mark Twain style. Kind of exaggerated correspondence.

MQPress: How did libraries contribute to your early career as a writer?

Smith: The way I kind of used the library, other than just a reference to find things, was when I would feel kind of dry or uninspired, I'd go to the Oak Park Library. I lived in Berwyn at the time. I'd go the Oak Park Library in any subject, finding some new books that I didn't have to buy. I'd take home from the library a stack of books. Some of them I never finished. But just having that outlet to get a bunch of books... it was almost like visiting a new country or having a new experience. And then it would revive me and I would get back into the groove. I would use the Chicago Historical Society's library where they have a lot of books you can't find anywhere else. The place in Lincoln Park. I did a lot of research about a guy named Captain Streeter.[36] Different Chicago subjects. For a while I was into a lot of Chicago stuff.

MQPress: What types of reading materials or books are in your personal book collection or library?

Smith: Lately, I have about two shelves of works about pre-Columbian cultures and the very earliest invasion of America by the Europeans which is very disgusting. I have a fairly large collection of poetry, of course. I have three or four shelves of Chicago literature from that period when I was studying Chicago literature. A shelf of suspense novels because I'm into reading Elmore Leonard and a bunch of other stuff.

MQPress: Besides libraries what other resources do you use to research your writing?

Smith: I only use the library, come to think of it, other than personal experience. I just use the libraries. I don't really use the Internet at all.

MQPress: What value do you believe libraries have to the general public?

Smith: There's so many different levels that libraries serve a community. It's a place where elderly people or lonely people go to be around books and around people. Most libraries, I think, have a young person place that's very accessible. Very different from when I was a kid. It's very kid-friendly and inspiring. What's great about it, In Chicago, at least, it's not just the intellectuals or people in the writing biz. Everyday people go there to figure out how to do things. Figure out about business. You see guys like me with a bag - the bookworm type. When you go to the library you see that it's really all kinds of people. The library's used by a lot of different people for a lot of different things.

MQPress: How have you used libraries for your latest work?

Smith: With this Native American stuff, I started at the library. You don't want to be buying books. So I would go to the library to find different volumes. Then I'd end up buying them because I wanted to keep them to use over and over again. I started by going to the library and testing different books about Native American culture to find out the direction I wanted to go. I started with the Black Hawk Wars.[37]

---

[36] George Wellington Streeter was a Mississippi riverboat captain whose *Reutan* ran aground near Superior Street in Chicago, Illinois in 1886. He remained on the sandbar, claimed the surrounding land, and defended it from developers and local authorities with force. Today, this upscale area of Chicago is known as Streeterville.

[37] Black Hawk, a subordinate chief of the Sauk and Fox, led five hundred warriors in warfare against white settlers of Illinois in 1832. His autobiography is considered an American classic.

Then I went back to the very beginning – [Christopher] Columbus chronicles and the [Hernando] De Soto chronicles. I found several books that I'm so happy I bought them on Ebay.

Hemingway's Writing Desk in Key West. Squirrelist

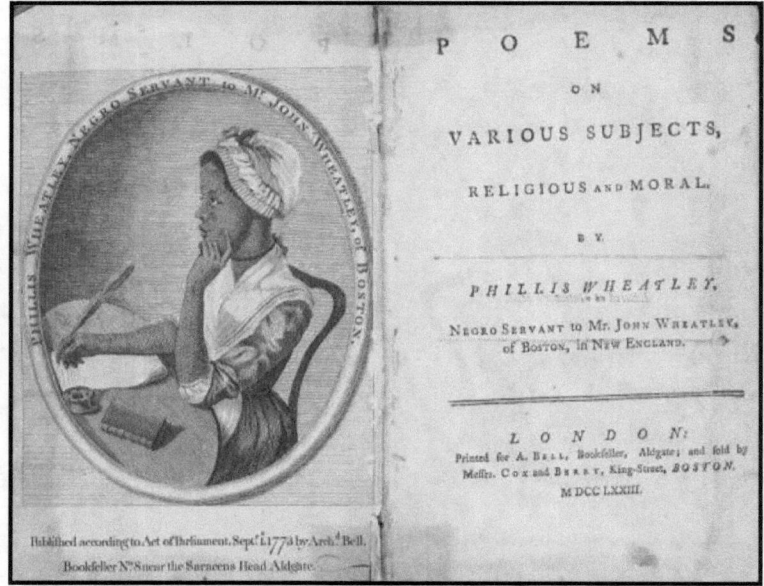

Frontispiece Image of Phyllis Wheatley Yale University

Chapter 4

Playwrights
&
Screenwriters

Play – Literary composition, in either verse or prose that tells a story through action and speech and is usually intended to be performed by actors before an audience. An element of theater.

Screenplay – Literary composition, usually prose that tells a story through action and speech and is usually intended to be performed by actors and recorded for mass reproduction.

Lydia Diamond

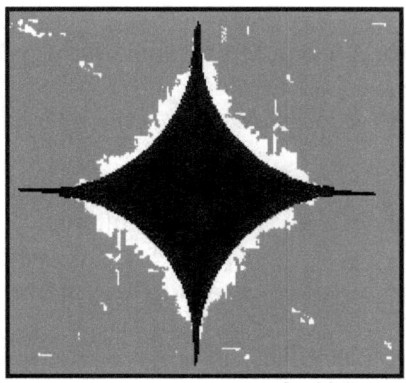

Lee McQueen

Lydia Diamond is a Huntington Playwriting Fellow and Resident Playwright at Chicago Dramatists. She taught playwrighting at Columbia College, DePaul University, Loyola University, and Boston University. She is contributing editor to *TriQuarterly*. Her plays include *Stage Black, The Gift Horse, Stick Fly,* and *The Inside.* She adapted *The Bluest Eye* to stage for Steppenwolf. A recent work is an adaptation of *Incidents in the Life of a Slave Girl.*

Telephone interview at New York City, NY. 2007

MQPress: Please describe your earliest experience as a library user, visitor, patron, or customer.

Diamond: That was when I was in school when I still lived in Amherst, Massachusetts. I went to grade school. Well even prior to that my mother was a university doctoral student. It was a good place for me to be sort of safe and comfortable and reading. The library was just somewhere to be sometimes. And then when I was at Wildwood School, in Amherst, Massachusetts, my middle school, the library was an amazing place to be because they had rabbits and all kinds of wonderful cuddly pets and of course great books. And pillows and wonderful places to sit. It was a positive environment. I remember the librarians being very kind. I remember thinking of the library as a place you'd want to spend time.

MQPress: How did libraries contribute to your early career as a writer?

Diamond: It's interesting. Because I sort of backed into my career as a writer. I was a theater major. I was studying to be an actor. My orientation to the library was sort of like most people's. It was doing research for school projects. The first time it related to my work as a writer was when I was in a class that did one-person shows. I was doing Nikki Giovanni. I remember doing some great research in the Northwestern University Library on Nikki Giovanni. The other thing I will say of my experience at Northwestern Library was there was a great librarian, Kathleen Bethel. One of the few African American adults with whom I could interact when I was in school at Northwestern.

MQPress: What types of reading materials or books are in your personal book collection or library?

Diamond: It's broad. I like reading novels. I would say primarily plays and novels. But then all genres, all kinds.

MQPress: Besides libraries, what other resources do you use to research your writing?

Diamond: I think it's probably mostly libraries. I do go online sometimes and look online and in online bookstores. But ultimately, they always sort of lead me to libraries.

MQPress: What value do you believe libraries have to the general public?

Diamond: I think the most exciting one, particularly in our very sort of consumer-driven society, is that they are free. I think that's amazing. And so that gives everyone sort of an equal footing in the library. You like to think at least equal access. I find that exciting to say the least. Also now that I'm a parent, the library is a community. You can take your kid there. And they can have a wonderful, stimulating place to be and things to do. And that's great too.

MQPress: How have you used libraries for your latest work?

Diamond: I wrote a play called *Voyeurs de Venus*. It had a production at Chicago Dramatists in Chicago last year. It was commissioned by Steppenwolf and produced by Chicago Dramatists. It won quite a few awards. It's actually about to have another production next summer at a theater in Virginia. That was a play about Saartjie Baartman, the woman who was [derogatively] referred to as Hottentot Venus.[38] And Kathleen Bethel actually helped me do the research for that. The same librarian that introduced me to the library when I was an undergraduate helped me with the research for that. That is the last, most recent, most tangible place the library has helped my research for a historical drama.

---

[38] "Ssehura" or "Saartjie Baartman" or "Sara" was born into the South African Khoe Khoe (Khoi Khoi) tribe, also known as the Quena people or "bushmen" in 1789. Already born with buttocks considered large by European standards, her genitals were enlarged through tribal ritual. In 1810, at the age of twenty, Baartman was sold to Europe and exhibited naked in a bamboo cage in London and Paris where she was called "The Hottentot Venus." She died in 1815 or 1816 of debatable causes – alcoholism, pleurisy, tuberculosis, small pox, or syphilis. After Baartman's death, her sexual organs and skeleton were preserved and displayed at Musee de l'Homme (Museum of Mankind) in Paris until 1976. At the official end of apartheid in 1994, Nelson Mandela formally requested France to return Baartman's remains to her traditional land. France granted Mandela's request in 2002.

Kirk Hanley

Brian McConley

Hanley has produced for Second City Chicago, but began with Second City Detroit. There, he served as actor and director of the Touring Company and actor/co-writer of four revues on the Detroit Mainstage. He also served as writer/actor/director/facilitator for Second City Communications. He co-wrote *Sex and the Second City* and *My Cousin's Wedding*. He has acted and written for children's theater, teen outreach programs, stage shows, improvisational comedy, television, radio, and film.

Telephone interview at Second City. Chicago, IL. 2007.

MQPress: Please describe your earliest experience as a library user, visitor, patron, or customer.

Hanley: Actually, I remember going to the library as a kid. I went to the library with a huge stack of books. You know, like twenty books that didn't look like I could ever read in the amount of time that I had to check them out. But usually I got through most of them. I tend to start a lot of books sometimes and not finish them. I remember that and I remember the school library. I can remember as a kid reading above my level. You read things that you think are gonna be fun as a kid. Especially *Alice in Wonderland.* They're very ahead of their time. Pretty hard for somebody and sometimes strange to understand. I do remember that. I remember this neighborhood library in Detroit where I grew up. I can remember the difference between the child's section and the adult's section. You couldn't read in the adult section until you were a certain age. I can't remember what the age was. Maybe ten-years-old. I just couldn't wait to get that library card. Getting into subjects that were more in-depth.

MQPress: How did libraries contribute to your early career as a writer?

Hanley: Well, I think when you're writing comedy theater you have to be a generalist. I think I've always been the kind of guy that read a lot of mysteries, read a lot of fiction, read a lot of non-fiction. Read about writing. Books on writing and all the different areas that you can contribute to as a writer.

MQPress: What types of reading materials or books are in your personal book collection or library?

Hanley: I've got a pretty good collection. Generally, they're the history of comedy. Comedy writing books. Books on general writing. Novel-writing. Screenplay-writing. Television-writing. Trivia and reference books. A few novels, but not very many. Generally, I tend toward the non-fiction in my home library. So I usually bite off more than I can chew. I see a book that I like and I buy it so that I can read it someday and then it sits on my shelf.

MQPress: Besides libraries, what other resources do you use to research your writing?

Hanley: Obviously, the Internet is terrific. Interviewing people live if there's a certain topic that you have or just experiencing life. When you're writing comedy, if you're writing sketch-based comedy,[39] you show people slices of life. Show people pieces of their life back in a comedic way. Sometimes in an exaggerated way. Sometimes in a very real way. It's just a combination of living life and being observant. And then also, obviously the Internet when you have something specific. It's a great resource. I'm forty-four this summer. I can remember a time before the Internet when it just wasn't possible to get certain pieces of information until they had written a book about it. It's amazing.

MQPress: What value do you believe libraries have to the general public?

Hanley: What value do they have to the general public? First of all, offering Internet access to people who wouldn't be able to afford it is a terrific resource that libraries offer. And then a chance to see a broad range of subjects, going to that Dewey Decimal range in the library, on writing or on personal finance. And kind of even at a glance to look at a couple of shelves and see sort of a range of knowledge, a range of ideas that are contained in a certain area is valuable. Obviously librarians as a resource are terrific if you don't even know how to frame the question that you want to ask. I've always found librarians to be very helpful

---

[39] Sketch comedy consists of a series of short comedy scenes. Such sketches are performed by a group of comedic actors, either on stage or through audio and/or visual means. Often, but not always, actors first improvise sketches then write them based upon the outcome of the improv sessions. Sketch comedy originated in vaudeville and music hall then moved to the stage. An important improvisational comedy scene developed in 1970s Chicago at Second City.

people. I think to the public they're a great resource. They are unique. It's a different experience than going to a book store. It's a communal place.

MQPress: How have you used libraries for your latest work?

Hanley: Well, if you're deciding to do a certain type of writing. I want to use humor or comedy writing in the greeting card industry. Rather than invest in books before knowing whether or not you'll be interested in them, you can check a couple of books out and get a general overview and then decide if that's the area you want to delve into. So I think it's a great resource tool to do that preliminary research into a topic. I do a lot of business theater writing. If you're writing for a finance company you can find those books in the library. Those types of things. When you're looking for something specific, when you're looking for that first level of knowledge they are a terrific resource.

♩　♩　♩　♩　♩　♩　♩　♩　♩　♩　♩　♩　♩　♩　♩

Matthew Porter

Matthew Porter

Porter has written for *Industry, Lifestyles, The Voyager,* and *The Door* magazines. He scripted *Blackwater Elegy* (95 Theses Entertainment), an award-winning short film starring Tony Award-winner John Cullum and Emmy-nominee Barry Corbin. He directed and produced *Jody Kerns: Southern Discomfort,* a live comedy concert video and *Stand Up Design,* a home design program. Besides film, he also writes for radio, television, and Internet programs.

Telephone interview at Winter Park, FL. 2007

MQPress: Please describe your earliest experience as a library user, visitor, patron, or customer.

Porter: That would take me back to when I was but a wee lad growing up in central Florida. I remember during the summer we would take trips pretty much every week to the library and come home with a stack of books. I would chew my way through those pretty quickly. It gave me a good foundation for what I would later build on to become a professional writer.

MQPress: How did libraries contribute to your early career as a writer?

Porter: Maybe from a technical/informational view they may help. But I think early on, more than anything, it stokes the fires of your imagination and your passion. Fiction and literature. There's technical things to be learned. But just having a deep desire to read and learn and absorb more information about the world around you... that's the driving force. The library as a resource is certainly useful. But it also fosters a passion for reading which is essential

MQPress: What types of reading materials or books are in your personal book collection or library?

Porter: It's very varied. We actually do have a library in our house. Not a huge house but it's important enough that we gave it its own room. We have everything from classic fiction – *Huckleberry Finn* and *On the Road* to recipe books, spiritual books. Just a little bit of everything. Science magazines. Just trying to build our own resource for us and for friends and for one day, children.

MQPress: Besides libraries what other resources do you use to research your writing?

Porter: Internet has been a huge resource in the last ten years. A lot of times there is some fact you need to double-check, or get a little more information, confirm spelling. It can put you in touch with other resources that can be of use. So the Internet is absolutely indispensable.

MQPress: What value do you believe libraries have to the general public?

Porter: I think it's an incredible, vital resource that puts virtually any book into the hands of folks without them having to buy it. It's not a modern invention, but it certainly enriches our lives even today. I think that it's an absolutely wonderful thing. I was at the library last night, as a matter of fact. That's how much I use it.

MQPress: How have you used libraries for your latest work?

Porter: I'm working with a new client right now, as a matter of fact. They're for the environment. I'm kind of reading up on some of the corporate culture. What's new in that world with Seth Godin and the whole *Purple Cow*[40] idea. *The World is Flat*. These kinds of books. I had a client who was developing a children's t.v. series. It was going to be based on fables. So I spent time going to the library checking out books on *Aesop's Fables* and *Grimm's Fairy Tales*. Just immersing myself in that world. It's a tremendous resource. And truly, even in the modern age, the library offers resources that you can't get in the same way on the Internet.

♩   ♩   ♩   ♩   ♩   ♩   ♩   ♩   ♩   ♩   ♩   ♩   ♩   ♩   ♩

---

[40] In *Purple Cow: Transform Your Business by Being Remarkable*, Seth Godin recommends that businesses and organizations who wish to be extraordinary rather than ordinary should do something remarkable rather than unremarkable in order to achieve success. In other words, the business should strive to be a purple cow in a field of brown cows.

Dylan Pritchett

McQueen Press

Prichett has been a full-time storyteller since 1990. His assembly program, *The Storyteller*, imparts valuable life lessons. Current president of the National Association of Black Storytellers, he teaches in the Kennedy Center's *Partners in Education* program. Author of the children's book, *The First Music*, and co-editor of the storyteller anthology, *Sayin' Somethin*,' he is part of *The Kings & Queens of Storytelling* video.

Interview at American Library Association Summer Meeting. Washington, DC. 2007

MQPress: Please describe your earliest experience as a library user, visitor, patron, or customer.

Pritchett: We're going back here. Way back in 19… As a matter of fact, I do have a very good first experience. In Williamsburg, Virginia we had this very, very, very small library. The first floor must have been ten feet by twenty feet. And then there were stairs that went up to the second floor and that was it. I used to go to the library on Saturday mornings to something called Fife and Drum. I was in the fife and drum corps[41] at Colonial Williamsburg. People have always seen the fifers and drummers walking the streets with their colonial costumes on. I was in that. When I was very young, ten or eleven, I remember going there and getting my library card. Every Saturday, I would take two books in and get two books out. And it was very interesting because I was the only Black person to ever use that library. And I never even thought about it until I was older why I never saw Black people using that library. I'll give the date. We're talking about 1969, 1970. So, in Virginia, integration had happened, but I just didn't see a lot of Black people using the library. It was very small. But I used it. And then when we got a larger library,

---

[41] Fife and drum is typically performed with a lead fife player, a vocalist, and drummers. The drum troop may include snare, tom, and bass. Originating in rural areas of the farming South, today fife and drum persists in Southern states. Performers play blues and gospel songs such as "When the Saints Go Marching In" and "When I Lay My Burden Down."

things kind of opened up. But it was a religion for me to go to that library and get a book on Saturday. That's probably where my love for reading started.

MQPress: How did libraries contribute to your early career as a writer?

Pritchett: Not. At. All. I'm only saying that because I'm kind of a late bloomer. Being a storyteller, I would write stories and just save them and use them to tell and not necessarily to write a book. And so, becoming an author is just something more so in the progression of becoming a storyteller more so than going to the library for research, etc. Because a lot of the stories that I've written have been written for years just waiting to be published. I'm sorry. That wasn't too good of an answer. But it's true.

MQPress: What types of reading materials or books are in your personal book collection or library?

Pritchett: Oh, I love Paul Laurence Dunbar. I have every book Paul Laurence Dunbar ever wrote. And I love Charles Chestnut. I like Negro dialect. On my fortieth birthday I bought for myself every volume of the ex-slave narratives. They're called *The American Experience*. People usually buy them for colleges or large library systems. But I wanted every volume. They're very expensive. They're $95 or $125 per volume. I bought all forty books. Because that was what I wanted to do. I read them. It's very difficult for me to read a novel. If a book is three to four hundred pages I won't finish it. It's probably my attention span. If there's a story that's longer than six pages, it's hard for me to get through. I like to read something quick and to think about it and to digest it. If a book is too long, I just don't tend to read it. But I love ex-slave narratives.[42] I just like reading dialect because that's how people talked. People don't talk how they write. I think with the ex-slave narratives, the writing is how people talked. And you don't find that. It's

---

[42] The slave or ex-slave narrative is a literary form that details the experiences of Africans enslaved in America. Approximately six thousand former slaves from North America and the Caribbean described their lives of servitude. About 150 were published as separate books or as pamphlets. Some such narratives are: *Life of William Grimes, the Runaway Slave* (1825), *The History of Mary Prince, a West Indian Slave* (1831), and *The Interesting Narrative and the life of Olaudah Equiano or Gustavus Vassa, the African* (1789). Narratives specifically written to inspire and encourage the abolition of slavery include Frederick Douglass's autobiography, *Narrative of the Life of Frederick Douglass* (1845), and *Incidents in the Life of a Slave Girl* (1861) by Harriet Jacobs. Stories written by white Americans or Europeans captured and enslaved in North Africa or by native populations in North America are commonly called captivity accounts.

a different flavor. That's really what I read. That's kind of odd because, you know, everybody has a favorite author. Someone mentioned an author that they were running to meet.

I said, "Who are they?"

"You don't know Judy Blah Blah?"

I said, "No, I don't know Judy Blah Blah. Who is Judy Blah Blah?"

They said, "Oh, she wrote so and so and so and so and so and so."

And I said, "Okay."

I don't read like that. And so, I think I'm very strange in that respect. Aren't I?

MQPress: Besides libraries what other resources do you use to research your writing?

Pritchett: Any kind of historical documents because I write about eighteenth nineteenth century African Americans. I don't necessarily write about the institution of slavery. But I write a lot about the plight of what folks did as well as African stories. I did a lot of research into African stories. I go into a lot of college libraries and find a lot of African stories that have been translated usually from the native language into English. Any kind of historical type of documentation is usually something that I'll use. I don't deal too much with fiction. I'll do the fantasy stuff in writing the story. But I want some facts to be able to have the factual information of the story correct.

MQPress: What value do you believe libraries have to the general public?

Pritchett: I think the library is invaluable because it is a place that you go to rather than using the computer to bring the information to you. I think that the biggest thing about a library has to do with the book. Has to do with being intimate with a book. Has to do with how you hold a book. How you smell a book. How a book talks to you. I think that's what libraries do. And there's a value to that. Children need to see that big people feel a book and hold a book. And there's a place to go to get a book. That nothing will ever take the place of a book. Not even a computer. It's more than just reading. There's a story that I'll share. It's a story that's in one of the ex-slave narratives. It's about a slave... and pardon me for saying slave... because it's about an enslaved person, who set the fire for his master. He would make sure the fire was going and he would extinguish the fire. And his master would sit, and as the account said, he would talk to his book. And so, what he was doing is what people do when they read. He would talk to his book. And this person would watch the master talk to his book. One night the master had finished reading. And he put him to bed and he noticed the book was still out. He went over to the bookshelf. Before he put the book up, he opened it. He said he closed the book and he opened it. He closed it and he opened it. He closed it again and he opened. He slammed the book and put it up on the shelf. And he said, "I don't know why the book didn't talk to me." It has to do with you talking to the book and the book talking to you. Fundamentals of reading. And that's the type of people society, children, we're raising when they don't talk to their book. When all they do is sit in front of a screen, they'll end up being screen people.

And when you say, "Have you read that book?"

"No."

"Well read the book."

"Well, the computer… "

"It's not the computer. Did you read the book?"

You have to have that intimate relationship with the book.

MQPress: How have you used libraries for your latest work?

[Note from Editor and Pritchett: The reader should see the answer to the fourth question]

♩   ♩   ♩   ♩   ♩   ♩   ♩   ♩   ♩   ♩   ♩   ♩   ♩   ♩   ♩

Libya Pugh

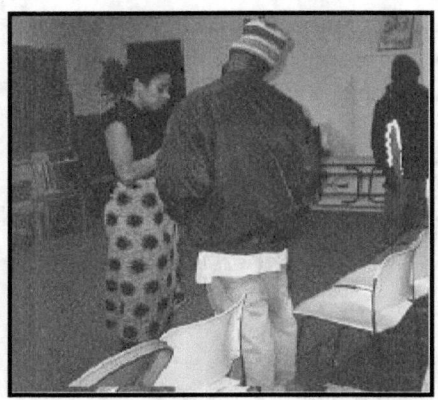

McQueen Press

Libya Pugh performed with the famous Steppenwolf Theater for *Wedding Band*, a collaboration with Congo Square. She appeared in *Piano Lesson, From the Mississippi Delta, As You Like It, and A Christmas Carol*. She has worked at ETA, Chicago Shakespeare, Lookingglass, St. Louis Repertory, Hope Summer Repertory, Milwaukee Shakespeare and Milwaukee Repertory. Her first work as playwright is the one-woman show, *Traveling Shoes*.

Interview at Bezazian Public Library. Chicago, IL. 2007

MQPress: Please describe your earliest experience as a library user, visitor, patron, or customer.

Pugh: The earliest experience was in second grade when I was a library helper and I learned the Dewey Decimal System. I became intrigued by the world of books around me. That was my first experience.

MQPress: How did libraries contribute to your early career as a writer?

Pugh: It motivated me to want to write. To be able to be in a library and have books readily available and computers to use to find them anywhere was intriguing to me. I continued to do that in my latter career as a writer.

MQPress: What types of reading materials or books are in your personal book collection or library?

Pugh: I have a variety of books. I have a lot of plays because I'm an actor. I have some fiction and non-fiction. But my favorite, I think, right now is biography. So I'm collecting biographies of different people.

MQPress: Besides libraries, what other resources do you use to research your writing?

Pugh: I use the Internet besides libraries. And Border's Bookstore.[43]

---

[43] Borders Group is an international bookseller based in Ann Arbor, Michigan and is the second-largest bookstore chain in the United States after Barnes & Noble.

MQPress: What value do you believe libraries have to the general public?

Pugh: I think it's like a dinosaur in some ways. It's the last place we can go that's free to get books without having to worry about finances and enjoy books. It's what makes us all Americans and all humans, that we're all able to share the same books.

MQPress: How have you used libraries for your latest work?

Pugh: I used the children's library for my latest work because I wanted to get right down to the point of the matter to write my play. They kind of skip over all of the complete history and talk specifically about what happened to these people. And so that's what I did.

♩　♩　♩　♩　♩　♩　♩　♩　♩　♩　♩　♩　♩　♩

Mike Wiley

McQueen Press

Mike Wiley Productions specializes in theatrical African American history narratives. With voice and posture, Wiley uses over a decade of acting experience to create real and fictional personalities from American history. Productions include *One Noble Journey, Jackie Robinson: A Game Apart, Brown vs. Board of Education, Tired Souls: King and the Untold Stories of the Montgomery Bus Boycott,* and *Dar He: The Lynching of Emmit Till.* Wiley also conducts youth programs and workshops.

Telephone interview at Mike Wiley Productions. Apex. NC. 2007

MQPress: Please describe your earliest experience as a library user, visitor, patron, or customer.

Wiley: My first experience with the library that had an effect on me was the fact that my mother was an assistant at the library in my hometown of Virginia. That library was in a pre-dominantly Black neighborhood so the librarians were Black and most of the patrons were Black. It was a wonderful family atmosphere at this library. It was a little, tiny library. I loved my time there. They always focused on positive influences in literature. Not just African American authors per se but people who were positive images who were writing about issues that the Black community was facing or that would interest people of my age. I was probably about, I don't know, eight or nine. I can still remember they would show, in the afternoon, they would show a film of some sort that had to do with education but was also fun. They would pop popcorn. This was back when there were no microwaves. The whole library would just fill with the smell of hot, buttered, off-the-stove popcorn. It was an experience that warms my heart to this day. The fact that my mother was a part of that means a lot to me.

MQPress: How did libraries contribute to your early career as a writer?

Wiley: When I was in junior high and doing research papers, I found that I could go and I could find magazines that were chock full of great quotes from people that I was interested in learning about. But not just learning about, but learning from. People like Robin Williams and Denzel Washington. Those kinds of individuals. I would look at their interviews in these magazines. Magazines that I wouldn't have been able to afford to get at home. Magazines like *Rolling Stone* or *Premiere* and then some autobiographies. Autobiographies that, of course, I probably wouldn't have bought at a bookstore because I just didn't buy books at that age. In looking at those interesting articles and reading those excerpts from books, it gave me the impetus to one day take those words of advice that I was getting from those particular periodicals and books and applying them to my own life and what I could do. I could get paid to be an actor. I could get paid to be a playwright. Eventually, I started visiting libraries not to learn about other individuals that were doing what I wanted to do, I started to visit libraries to *do* what those individuals were doing. And that is write plays. Libraries have become an invaluable resource when it comes to being able to do the things that I do. Because the plays I write are documentary-style plays. I take true stories and I dramatize them. Where's the best place to find a true story and information about individuals, especially the individuals that I write about who are usually African American or an event from African American history? What better place to find that information than the library?

MQPress: What types of reading materials or books are in your personal book collection or library?

Wiley: I'd say that as far as non-fiction goes, I have some David Sedaris, some Eric Bogosian.[44] Individuals that are artists as well as performers. I would suppose you'd call them performance artists. But I also have plays in my collection as well as books about acting and instructional books about playwriting and biographies about individuals. Not just African Americans but performers and artists. My wife is a zoologist so our collection is part scientific and part artistic. So we have many books about baboons and the training of animals while at the same time we have books about actors and the training of human beings.

MQPress: Besides libraries what other resources do you use to research your writing?

Wiley: Documentary films. Plays. Some bookstores, but I find it's easier to use the library because I don't want to necessarily own a book unless I'm always going to go back to it over the course of several years. So I don't find that I use bookstores as much as I use libraries to find my

---

[44] Eric Bogosian is an actor, playwright, and performance artist. David Sedaris is a humorist and playwright.

materials for plays. If I don't use the library, I'm going to use some other form or place to find that material such as other films or plays, documentaries, newspapers, and first person accounts. Oral histories[45] are the bottom line for me. Oral history, or if I can get some commentary or quote from some person in a first-hand account on whatever I'm writing about, that is golden to me.

MQPress: What value do you believe libraries have to the general public?

Wiley: I would say overall, libraries level the playing field because they allow people who can't afford to buy books the opportunity to still read, to still be a part of whatever dialogue might be going on in the country as far as a book or subject matter is concerned. Because they don't have to be part of the elite society that goes out and can afford to purchase a novel or a biography or a work of fiction or non-fiction that they might be talking about on *Oprah* or in the news. A few years ago, *Primary Colors*[46] came out. If we didn't have libraries, there would be a great portion of society who would have no idea of what this book is about that they keep talking about on the news. I can't afford to go to a bookstore and buy it. Luckily our society has public libraries where we can go and get books without a charge. And if we can't afford to go overseas we can read about going overseas. If we can't afford to have our deck remodeled we can read about how to remodel it ourselves. Libraries have a hand in making their lives better.

MQPress: How have you used libraries for your latest work?

Wiley: I actually use more research libraries for my latest work. Currently, I'm adapting a book called [*Love in the Time of Cholera*]. I found that there are newspaper accounts and videos and audio samplings that I can't get in a bookstore. I can only get them from the library. The library has been quite a valuable source and tool for me to find the material that I need on a daily basis. That's one thing I do not want to do is have to visit a bookstore to buy little bits and pieces. Because that's, in essence, what I'm having to do… take little pieces here and little pieces there and put them together… little pieces of primary source documents or quotes

---

[45] Oral history involves the recording or transcribing of eyewitness accounts of historical events. Historians, folklorists, anthropologists, sociologists, and journalists employ interviews in their research. Oral historians maintain common ethics and standards of practice, particularly "informed consent" of persons being interviewed.

[46] *Primary Colors* is a 1996 novel written by "Anonymous," later identified as Joe Klein, a journalist. The fictional account is widely understood to be a *roman à clef* (a novel that describes real events behind a façade of fiction) inspired by former U.S. President, William Jefferson Clinton's 1992 presidential campaign.

or oral histories. Putting them all together to make one big story and make it flow. It's so much easier to just go to the library, photocopy, or read a piece of material, and then fit it where it needs to go within my play rather than buying the whole book and hoping that I can use one hundred percent of the book or ninety-nine percent of the book or even seventy-five percent of the book… and then getting it home and realizing… I have a lot of books in my collection that I bought thinking that I was going to use them on a regular basis and they just sort of sit and collect dust.

⌐ ⌐ ⌐ ⌐ ⌐ ⌐ ⌐ ⌐ ⌐ ⌐ ⌐ ⌐ ⌐ ⌐ ⌐

The Librarian, 1556.   Giuseppe Arcimboldo

Chapter 5

Non-Fiction
Writers
&
Essayists

Non-fiction - A work is presented as fact, meaning the work can be proven true or proven false. Essays, journals, documentaries, scientific papers, photographs, biographies, and textbooks are some examples of non-fiction.

Essay – Literary form defined as an expository piece of prose. Informs and explains rather than dramatizes and creates. Achieves effect by direct statement rather than using imaginary characters to act out a situation. Usually confined to a particular aspect of a subject from the writer's own point of view.

Zaid Abdul-Aziz

McQueen Press

Zaid Abdul-Aziz is a former professional basketball player who starred at Iowa State University. Drafted by the Cincinnati Royals in 1968, he was also a member of the Milwaukee Bucks, Seattle Super Sonics, Houston Rockets, Buffalo Braves, and Boston Celtics. *Darkness to Sunlight: The Life-Changing Journey of Zaid Abdul-Aziz* ("Don Smith") is his autobiography released by Sunlight Publishing in partnership with Baker & Taylor and QBI.

Interview at American Library Association Mid-Winter Meeting. Seattle, WA. 2007

MQPress: Please describe your earliest experience as a library user, visitor, patron, or customer.

Abdul-Aziz: I grew up in Brooklyn, New York. I was born in the Bedford-Stuyvescent area of that city. If I would have known that I would be a writer, I would have never believed it. As a young child, I didn't like the library. I didn't want to have anything to do with it. My earliest experience in the library was at Iowa State University. I took a one-credit course in library and library systems. I had to do a bibliography. I hated it. It was one of the hardest courses I had taken. But I was able to publish a book.

MQPress: How did libraries contribute to your early career as a writer?

Abdul-Aziz: It's the isolation. I began my book about three and a half years ago. It's called *Darkness to Sunlight*. It's published by Sunlight Inc. What it did for me was give me isolation. I was able to isolate and find a room in the library. The library that I worked at was Shoreline Library which I spoke at on Thursday, January 18th. Also, they have the Internet which helped me a lot. They had word-processing. You could print out about seventy-five pages a week.

MQPress: What types of reading materials or books are in your personal book collection or library?

Abdul-Aziz: I have autobiographies. I'm not like a fiction guy or a science fiction guy. I like to read about people's lives or stories that have a message. One of my favorite books is a book by John Hershey called *White Lotus*. It was pretty much done in first person narrative. I read *The Catcher in the Rye* when I was in college. I began reading that again. Also, I was very impressed by a book by Edward P. Jones called *Lost in the City*. It's about his experiences in Washington, D.C. One story in particular that really touched me was a story called *The Girl Who Loved Pigeons*. Which was very touching to me.

MQPress: What other resources do you use to research your writing?

Abdul-Aziz: I also go to places like Barnes & Noble.[47] You can take any book and take it to a table and do research on it. I've done that at Barnes & Noble. I've been to Borders. Also, there's a place I used to go to called the Work Source. Funny enough, it was a place where people are looking for jobs. I used to go in there and use their facilities. As a matter of fact, the manager of Work Source came to a reading that I did night. Those were some of the things I did to augment my writing.

MQPress: What value do you believe libraries have to the general public?

Abdul-Aziz: The value is just enormous. First thing, you can go in there and use the Internet, get on a computer. You can get just about any book you want. Sometimes it takes time for them to get a book in. Normally, in about three or four days, you get whatever you need. They have a great system here in Seattle. I spoke on July 15, 2006. I did the inaugural opening of the library at Northgate here. Like I said, on Thursday, the other day, I spoke at the Shoreline Library. I don't know how they are in other places, but I'm really impressed with being able to go in and have the librarians help me the way that they did especially in the state of Washington.

MQPress: How have you used libraries for your latest work?

Abdul-Aziz: I had to gather permissions to be able to use some of the photos and permissions to use certain material in my book.[48] I used the libraries a lot for that purpose. Of course, the Internet is just invaluable

---

[47] Barnes & Noble, Inc. is the largest bookstore chain in the United States with its headquarters in New York City.

[48] When a person has permission, that person is allowed to use certain work that belongs to another person. Permission is often (but not always) required because of intellectual property laws that protect creative works such as text, artwork, photographs, or music. If a person uses a copyrighted or trademarked work without appropriate permission, that person may violate or "infringe" the owner's rights to that work. Infringing someone else's rights may subject the infringer to legal action, including orders to cease and desist or payment of financial damages.

to me. I'm the type of writer that likes to write everything out in longhand. That way it looks more personal to me and has more meaning for me than typing it out. I have to type it out anyway. Sometimes I go, 'I didn't write that.' But knowing I did write it. It's right in front of me in longhand. So the library, being able to go in and use the word processor, being able to get feedback from the librarians on what I'm working on at that time is just an enormous help for me as a writer.

♩　♩　♩　♩　♩　♩　♩　♩　♩　♩　♩　♩　♩　♩

Jeff Angus

Angus has a career in management, sports writing, entrepreneurship, information technology, and business consulting. He's worked with State of Illinois, The Data Works, Farallon Computing, *InfoWorld*, and *InformationWeek*. He's written for *XML Magazine*, *PC World*, *Computerworld*, *New York Times*, *Washington Post*, and *Seattle Times*. His latest work is *Management by Baseball: The Official Rules for Winning Management in Any Field*.

McQueen Press

Interview at American Library Association Mid-Winter Meeting. Seattle, WA. 2007

MQPress: Please describe your earliest experience as a library user, visitor, patron, or customer.

Angus: I've always been a library rat. I always hung out in libraries. I found it really fascinating. I would sneak out of class sometimes in my school and I would read the encyclopedia. I started with C and read through D and E when I was in elementary school. I just loved it.

MQPress: How did libraries contribute to your early career as a writer?

Angus: It's kind of indirect. Books, reading contributed. And, of course, libraries are a way to be exposed. Especially non-computerized card catalogs. When I was growing up they weren't computerized. The serendipity of searching for a book and then finding others and making notes to myself and reading things that I've blundered across while looking for other things, it's just beautiful.

MQPress: What types of reading materials or books are in your personal book collection or library?

Angus: I have so many books. My wife was a bookseller. And so, between us, we're both really book people. We met over books. I have a couple thousand titles. She has a couple thousand titles. We had to build built-in book shelves to accommodate them all. We'd buy book shelves. We have everything. I'd say a little bit over half non-fiction. But we have tons of fiction.

MQPress: Besides libraries, what other resources do you use to research your writing?

Angus: I use the Internet to some degree. I'm very skilled at it. I've been doing that for a long time. But, frankly, I prefer physical books to electronic pages. I do a lot of interviews of human beings who are libraries of experiences.

MQPress: What value do you believe libraries have to the general public?

Angus: They're indispensable. They're indispensable on a strategic high level and on a tactical level. So in the big picture, you cannot have a democracy without a well-educated and well-rounded citizenry. Libraries are the heart of that process. They pump knowledge through the system. Little branch libraries are the foundation of so many people discovering not only things they need to know but things that are worthwhile knowing even though they don't need to know them. To me, on a global level, you cannot have a functioning democracy without an active and vibrant library system. But books are kind of expensive, in our country, anyway. We've made a decision to reduce people's income relative to cost. Inflation and books have gone up faster than people's wages.[49] For example, I'm an active book-buyer, but I cannot afford to buy everything I want. So I heavily use the library. If I'm really pleased with a book, I go out and buy it. So I use it on that tactical level to figure out what can I afford to buy.

MQPress: How have you used libraries for your latest work?

Angus: Of course, I use libraries. I'm fortunate. I live in Seattle, Washington. We have a good collection. Of course, there are inter-library loans. One of the best things about Seattle Public Library - I wish all libraries had this – is we have a quick information desk. You can call and talk to a reference librarian pretty quickly and get an amazing range.

---

[49] Factors such as book size, paper quality, number of books printed, illustrations, printer negotiations, and storage all affect the production costs of a book. However, costs include not only paper, printing, and binding, but also staff overhead, promotion, distribution, and returns policy. The author also gets a percentage. The market trend towards quality trade paperback as opposed to mass-market paperback affects book price. Finally, mass conglomeration versus private ownership in the publishing industry brings into focus the industry's obligation to its stockholders which affects book price. These many factors affect the retail price which impacts the consumer. In response, consumers have found solutions or alternatives such as use of library resources, access to online used book catalogs to find used books, and the choice of "big box" retailers instead of traditional bricks and mortar bookstores. For a fuller analysis, refer to "Why Do Books Cost So Much" written by Christopher Dreher on December 3, 2002 for Salon.com at http://dir.salon.com/story/books/feature/2002/12/03/prices.

You always get somebody who loves finding things out. Good reference librarians[50] are always like that. But I notice that there are fewer and fewer of them.[51] I don't know where they keep them now. I don't blunder across them as often as I used to.

⌐ ⌐ ⌐ ⌐ ⌐ ⌐ ⌐ ⌐ ⌐ ⌐ ⌐ ⌐ ⌐ ⌐ ⌐

---

[50] Reference [see Glossary of Library Terms].
[51] Some reasons for dwindling numbers of librarians include (1) retirement, (2) downsizing, (3) burnout and (4) very low pay compared to other professions requiring education at the Master level.

Alan Axelrod

McQueen Press

Axelrod has served as a history consultant for museums, *The Wild West* (A&E), and *Civil War Journal* (Discovery Channel). A prolific writer, *Downbeat*, *South Carolina Review*, *American Studies*, and *Fortune* feature his work. Though his specialties are military history and the American West, he also writes on astronomy, jazz, bartending, and folklore. Some works include: *Patton on Leadership*, and *Elizabeth I, CEO*.

Interview at American Library Association Summer Meeting. Washington, DC. 2007

MQPress: Please describe your earliest experience as a library user, visitor, patron, or customer.

Axelrod: My earliest experience was, I suppose, I was five or six-years-old. It was the Austin Branch of the Chicago Public Library in the west side of Chicago. It seemed to me a kind of palace. It was a great place with big French doors. The amazing thing was they gave you books for free. All through my childhood I would either visit that library or a bookmobile that would come by, I think once every two weeks. It was a kind of ritual to go in the bookmobile and find some books. The books that I really loved was book about building things - electronic things. When I really loved a book, my mother would try to find it for me and buy it for me. It was a great place.

MQPress: How did libraries contribute to your early career as a writer?

Axelrod: I think, mostly as a kind of inspiration. You walk through the stacks of a library and you want to be part of it. You want to get yourself in those shelves somewhere. When I went to graduate school at the University of Iowa, the first thing I did was go to the library. I walked among the stacks of the dissertations. I thought I could be one of these and contributed to this body of knowledge. The library is essentially an inspiration. And, of course, you have access to books you either can't afford or can't possibly get anymore to own. As I've made a real career in writing I try to buy as many books I need as I possibly can. I like to have them. But my own personal library will never replace a public university library.

MQPress: What types of reading materials or books are in your personal book collection or library?

Axelrod: All sorts, but especially history and military history. I tend to buy books that I am going to use in writing my own books. I started out life as an English professor so I have a lot of literature. But as I've gotten older I tend to specialize much more in acquiring non-fiction.

MQPress: Besides libraries what other resources do you use to research your writing?

Axelrod: I use a lot of military archives and also the Internet. That's something you've got to be pretty careful with. But there are amazing resources on it. Particularly, archival resources. A lot of historical information has been scanned. At the very least, it can point you in the direction of a print resource if you can't get the whole resource online.

MQPress: What value do you believe libraries have to the general public?

Axelrod: Well, they're the soul of any city. You can't have a real community without a library. I think they're the heart and soul of any city. They're places to get kids interested. I think they're a real statement of value of what the community thinks is important.

MQPress: How have you used libraries for your latest work?

Axelrod: As resources for mainly books that I could not readily obtain. For instance, I'm working on a book about a fellow named George Creel who was an American propagandist in World War I. A number of his own books I've only been able to find in the main branch of the Atlanta Public Library where I live. So it's been very valuable to me. I also use libraries when I'm writing to sort of test out sources that I'm going to use to see if it's worth investing in so that I can own it.

Timuel D. Black, Jr.

McQueen Press

World War 2 veteran, Timuel D. Black Jr., is Professor Emeritus of the City Colleges of Chicago. He taught history and social studies in Chicago public schools. He is author of *Bridges of Memory: Chicago's First Wave of Black Migration*, an oral history of African Americans who migrated from the South to Chicago. *Bridges of Memory Volume 2: Chicago's Second Generation of Black Migration* is his latest work.

Interview at Woodson Regional Library. Chicago, IL. 2007[52]

MQPress: Please describe your earliest experience as a library user, visitor, patron, or customer.

Black: I have used the library as a source of information since I was about eight or nine years old. Even earlier than that. Before the Hall Library at 48th and Michigan. My mother and father, my mother mostly, would take us to the library that was on Grand Boulevard called Forestville. Then they would take us downtown to the main library – that was in the building where the Chicago Cultural Center is now. And so in my early experiences there was always the library. I was very glad and it was very helpful to see young people like myself. So the library became a way of doing two things for me. And that was being by myself and enjoying what I was doing, reading. And getting information that otherwise would not be available with just talking to people.

MQPress: How did libraries contribute to your early career as a writer?

Black: Well, very much so. In the elementary schools as well as high school, the teachers were very, very persuasive in getting us to use the library. So much so that in the summertime, we would not just use the neighborhood library. We would roller-skate downtown to the main library on Randolph which is now the Cultural Center. 1932-33. We could get books and bring them back home and keep them until the end of summer. The local library in my neighborhood, which came into

---

[52] Black completed by telephone the interview that began in-person at Woodson.

being in 1932 or 1933, was the George Cleveland Hull Library, located at 48th and Michigan. That was what we might call kind of a hangout. We would read what we wanted to read and talk about what we read. That continued on through high school. I learned to do primary research at DuSable High School under the instruction of the late, great Mary Herrick who was a first-rate intellectual as well as a great teacher. That was a continuation of the library being a major resource of information. Then of course, during the Great Depression, many of the outstanding Blacks such as Langston Hughes or W.E.B. Dubois would come to our neighborhood. The George Cleveland Hull Library would be the place where they would come to give lectures. Help us young people to appreciate information.

MQPress: What types of reading materials or books are in your

Black: In my library, there's an accumulation of about two thousand. Most of it is about Black life all over the world. Some of it is fun reading. All kinds but mostly academic and research material. Most of them are not novels. Maybe fiction that deals with social issues. Of course magazines as well. Magazines about race and class and gender. Just a broad spectrum of books in my library.

MQPress: Besides libraries, what other resources do you use to research your writing?

Black: Much of it would be in the university libraries. University of Chicago. Roosevelt University. University of Illinois. Both Champaign-Urbana as well as Chicago. And being on the scene during the Civil Rights Movement and before that organizing the Blacks on the Southside into unions. I would say primarily people that I associate with. To listen to them and to sometimes ask certain kinds of questions. You may know that I have two volumes out. Oral histories called *Bridges of Memory* which deals with three generations of people who grew up in Chicago taken in the context of social anthropology. People that I've talked with are a source of information. I use interviews and personal conversations. And checking out with scholars, information I might have read about. I get confirmation whether they agree with what I'm writing about. Then just observing behavior. For example, if I was going to write about the neighborhood where I live, Hyde Park-Kenwood. I could walk around that neighborhood and see the physical condition of the housing, the shopping, what resources are available. Then I could describe that neighborhood in maybe complimentary terms. But then, if I want to make a comparison, I'd walk just west of that neighborhood. And I see something dramatically different. Then I could write about those kinds of contrasts of the two, side by side, almost villages.

MQPress: What value do you believe libraries have to the general public?

Black: Fantastic. There are various forms of electronic and other equipment. Technology which libraries can afford to have but ordinary homes wouldn't have. Libraries even now are more important, but used less, unfortunately than they used to be.

MQPress: How have you used libraries for your latest work?

Black: For the oral histories, it wasn't necessary. In the latest work in terms of the volumes of *Bridges of Memory* there hasn't been too much use of the libraries as such except for what I have personally in my own library at home. The public library has not been used as a big source except we now have archives developed of many of my materials at The Vivian Harsh archives in the Carter G. Woodson Regional Library at 95th and Austin. That is another way of using the library. This is a kind of energy between my own materials and the Vivian Harsh Collection. We're encouraging more young people to use the library more. And look at the archives of people who grew up in Chicago so they learn how to use primary resource materials. But in the past when I've done research, I used the library as much as possible as a primary source area. I tried to get the original documents as they were put out by the person that created the document. So the library is a very important place for writers to go and do documentary research. What I've done here is not documentary. This is personal. Person-to-person. What we call in anthropological terms, participant-observer[53] kind of thing. So that's what this is about. The library is an important part. And people can take this book and check out what those people have said in the library.

---

[53] Participant observation is a research strategy used in the fields of sociology and anthropology which provides familiarity with a group of individuals (a community or subculture) and their practices in their own environment. The method has its origins in the field work of social anthropologists like Bronisław Malinowski in Britain, Franz Boas in the US, and the University of Chicago's School of Sociology. Research methods include: informal interviews, direct observation, participation in the life of the group, collective discussions, analyses of personal documents, self-analysis, and oral histories.

Claire Buchwald

McQueen Press

Buchwald is director of Focus Interactive Research which assists organizations with evaluation, project management, team-building, writing, public relations, and strategic planning. Her writings include research reports, curriculum, training manuals, and proposals like *Building Cultural Responsiveness in Minnesota's Childcare System*. She wrote *Are You Ready for Me?*, *The Puppet Book*, *The Mitzvah-Go-Round*, and co-wrote *Max Talks to Me*.

Interview at American Library Association Summer Meeting. Washington, DC. 2007

MQPress: Please describe your earliest experience as a library user, visitor, patron, or customer.

Buchwald: Well, I grew up in Edina, Minnesota. My mother took us to the library every week. I remember how thrilling it was when I got my first library card with my very own signature on there and everything. I was seven-years-old. Since then, I've made it a special experience for my own children called Reading Day. Read as much as I wanted. Then when I was a little older, I would get out about seven to eight books at a time for five to seven days. I couldn't stand to finish it so quickly so I would start another book. I would alternate those books to make each one last longer. I will never forget the experience of going there.

MQPress: How did libraries contribute to your early career as a writer?

Buchwald: Well, first of all, for inspiration. I couldn't buy all the books that I read. I bought almost none of the books that I read because I was reading about a book a day. To be able to go to the library to read all of these books was very inspiring. My mother is also an author so I would get to hear her read her books at the library. That was wonderful. Then libraries contributed to my early career too and they do now. Because at a library, one can check out who's publishing books on certain themes and who does the most beautiful or wonderful books of the sort one wants to do. And then one knows who to send their work to.

MQPress: What types of reading materials or books are in your personal book collection or library?

Buchwald: Thousands of children's books, literally, and including now quite a few picture books. Because I have three young children – nine, seven, and three. We read quite a bit everyday. But I've always liked children's and young adult literature. Now, I'm starting to read mysteries as well. Including dog mysteries and books about women who have something to do with dogs as a trainer and also solve mysteries. Those are a lot of fun.

MQPress: Besides libraries what other resources do you use to research your writing?

Buchwald: Now I use the Internet quite a bit. I find it very useful to do research whether it's on publishers or the subject matter to begin with.

MQPress: What value do you believe libraries have to the general public?

Buchwald: I think they are some of the greatest resources we have in this country. I was shocked in 1986, 1987 when I was studying in Italy and I went to the library. I always thought of libraries as places that were easy to use, accessible, user-friendly places. But the library there was nothing like that. There was no children's library. There was no browsing library. You had to know what you wanted. Had to use an old-fashioned card catalog[54] then write down what you wanted. And then wait in line. They would go back to stacks and bring back what you wanted if it was available. Then you had only a certain amount of time to use it *in the library*. You needed all kinds of special identification in order to be able to check out anything at all. We as visitors, as students studying there, we couldn't get that special identification. So we couldn't check any books out of the library. And even to get things copied, one had to stand in another line and then pay for copy service and come back - you couldn't get them the same day - come back another day to get them. And then I really realized how precious it is to be able to have access to all kinds of books no matter who you are.

MQPress: How have you used libraries for your latest work?

Buchwald: Well, my latest works are about dogs. There's one about the relationship between a dog and his boy. And another one called *Are You Ready For Me?* about how to decide whether your family and a dog are right for each other. I really did use libraries and also the Internet in researching *Are You Ready For Me?* because I wanted to know what

---

[54] Card catalog [see Glossary of Library Terms].

resources were out there that I could refer people to at the end of the book. With *Max Talks to Me*, I needed to learn more about the different ways dogs communicate. I knew from my own experience but I wanted to learn from animal experts, dog experts. And so, where did I turn to? Of course to books. And where did I find the books? In the library.

♩　♩　♩　♩　♩　♩　♩　♩　♩　♩　♩　♩　♩　♩　♩

Anthony Chiffolo

Anthony Chiffolo has written several books including *100 Names of Mary: Stories and Prayers,* and *Advent and Christmas with the Saints.* He has served as editor and compiler for *In my Own Words: Pope John Paul II, Pope John XXIII: In My Own Words* and *At Prayer with the Saints.* He co-authored *We Thank You, God, For These: Blessings and Prayers for Family Pets.* Currently, he is editorial director for Praeger Publishers. His latest work is the popular *Cooking with the Bible.*

Interview at American Library Association Mid-Winter Meeting. Seattle, WA. 2007

MQPress: Please describe your earliest experience as a library user, visitor, patron, or customer.

Chiffolo: The first library experience I really remember is probably when I was in middle school although I don't exactly remember the grade or the age. I had to write a paper for history or social studies. I decided to research the Sacco and Vanzetti Trial.[55] And so I remember going to the library and doing the research. That's my first recollection. There may have been times earlier, I'm sure, when I was younger just going to the library. That's what I remember

MQPress: How did libraries contribute to your early career as a writer?

Chiffolo: The first book I wrote was called *At Prayer with the Saints.* It's an anthology, a collection of prayers composed by the saints themselves. I went to the library at Saint Louis University. Looking through the old books that they had in their collection. Searching through to find the prayers that had been written by saints from the early centuries up to the present. The collection there at Saint Louis University was very good.

---

[55] Sacco and Vanzetti, two Italian American laborers and anarchists, were tried, convicted, and executed in 1927 for armed robbery and murder. Mass national and international protests took place throughout the legal proceedings. To this day, the actual guilt or innocence of both men remains a source of controversy amid revelations of judicial misconduct and mishandled evidence.

It's a Roman Catholic school and they have a lot of material on the saints. Since I happened to be living in that area at the time, it was very convenient.

MQPress: What types of reading materials or books are in your own personal book collection or library?

Chiffolo: I have a lot of books on the saints and on religion and spirituality. I also have a number of art books, some books about some of my favorite artists and photographers. I am an amateur photographer. And nature guide books as well.

MQPress: Besides libraries what other resources do you use to research your writing?

Chiffolo: Besides libraries, I use the Internet a lot, looking through the various websites in order to find information. I also will order books through Amazon to purchase a book if I need to use it. So those would be the sources.

MQPress: What value do you believe libraries have to the general public?

Chiffolo: Well I use libraries still for my own personal purposes. I go to my local library and I take out books-on-tape because I have a rather long commute. So I listen to books as I'm driving to and from work. I see a lot of people doing that. I have also checked out videos from the library. Things I never saw when they were at the theater. So I bring them home and watch them at my leisure on my schedule. Occasionally, nowadays, I check out a book just to read, a novel. I see, when I go to the library, a lot of people going there to get books-on-tape and videos. Also going there to get books on things that affect them like books on health, finances. And then of course I see that the children's section of the library is always very busy. Parents bring their children in to introduce them to the library as well but also to learn to use the library and its references. So I think it's very important for people to have a place to go so they can get this information. Especially at the larger libraries, they subscribe to a lot of databases.[56] People go in and they use the databases sometimes even more than they'll look through the books in the stacks. So that's an important resource as well.

MQPress: How have you used libraries for your latest work?

Chiffolo: The latest book was *Cooking with the Bible*. That involved a lot of research in a lot of different areas. That covers, of course, a very long period, two thousand years or more. Researching the history of the scripture and its translations as it has come down to us. Researching the

---

[56] Database [see Glossary of Library Terms].

history of the foods and the ingredients that we used in the book. So there were a lot of different searches done looking for history of food books. Looking for daily life books. How did people live in the time of the Egyptian pharaohs? What were their food preparation methods? What foods did they eat? What ingredients did they have access to? That sort of thing. Looking for information about how the scriptures have been translated and how they have been corrupted in the translations, looking at some of the originals. We used the libraries for all of that. As well, we have been lucky to be able to make presentations at the library after the book has been published. So we had a night, for example, where we went and spoke to a group of about thirty people. We prepared a couple of recipes – dessert recipes because it was after dinner. And we spoke to the people about the book and some of the things we learned, some of the surprising things that we had discovered. We allowed them to taste some of the spices that we used which were new and unfamiliar to them and to taste some of the recipes we prepared. Gave them a kind of overview. So yes. It was a nice event. It was a nice thing for a library to do. It's a very easy type of thing for a library to put on. We've enjoyed the relationship that we've had with libraries.

♩   ♩   ♩   ♩   ♩   ♩   ♩   ♩   ♩   ♩   ♩   ♩   ♩   ♩

Rosie Molinary

Deborah Triplett

Molinary's poetry and non-fiction have been published in *The Circle*, *Caketrain*, *Snake Nation Press*, *Jeopardy*, *Coloring Book*, and *Waking Up American*. She writes for *Ms*, *Health*, and *Women's Health*. She teaches self-awareness, creativity, social justice, and writing at continuing education programs, schools, colleges, conferences, and nonprofits. Her first book, *Hijas Americanas* (Seal Press), shows how strongly culture affects self-image and lifestyle.

Telephone interview at Davidson, North Carolina. 2007

MQPress: Please describe your earliest experience as a library user, visitor, patron, or customer.

Molinary: The library was probably my greatest indulgence. Every Saturday I had a trip to the library. I was allowed to take as long as I wanted. If I took four hours, that was fine. If I took four minutes, it was fine. It was so affirming for me as a reader to be indulged in that way. I was the kind of kid who stayed up real late at night with a flashlight under the blanket reading a book or taking it to the dinner table and kind of putting it in my lap to read and pushing the boundaries little bit further. I know that my love for books and writing were absolutely inspired by my dad's support of my initial interest.

MQPress: How did libraries contribute to your early career as a writer?

Molinary: My career as a fulltime writer is young. And so my early career is not that long ago. I most used the library when I was doing my book research. Very early on I set up an appointment with the librarian. I let her know what I was looking for. That was good guidance on how I could use the university library to find the most relevant research on the topic.

MQPress: What types of reading materials or books are in your personal book collection or library?

Molinary: It continues to be my indulgence. I would rather buy a book than anything else. Almost every time I go into the book store I come out with an embarrassment of riches. So what type of books do I have? I have everything from fiction to non-fiction. Books on craft. I really enjoy reading non-fiction, I think, because I write non-fiction and as I read, I'm not just reading stories for insight. I'm also learning for me and the craft woman. So that's what I read a lot of. Right now there's a basket of books in my office that are the books that are slotted for next. That basket probably has forty books in it if not more. I still have plenty other stuff I want to get to. I tend to be a book buyer now because I don't want to have to go when I'm done.

MQPress: Besides libraries what other resources do you use to research your writing?

Molinary: Easily the Internet a good bit. One of the things that I like to do at the college or university library is go through the journals that they have and see what articles are in there. And then maybe learn about those studies and track down those researchers and then arrange [to meet] with them. So I find the library in terms of research, is still a really great place for me because I know where to find more based on Internet. The Internet usually leads me to direct primary sources. I also like to use the library when I'm writing about a field that I need to know about when I write fiction which isn't often. But let's say I have a firefighter in there. I'd like to go to the library to find books on firefighting so I can have that frame of reference before I talk to a fireman or go along on a ride.

MQPress: What value do you believe libraries have to the general public?

Molinary: It's the tools or the link. And it was reading and writing. Reading allowed me to expand my sense of possibilities. It gave me exposure to things I probably wouldn't have written any other way. So I could learn what it was like in hair salon in Afghanistan. What it's like to adopt a little girl from China. Or what it's like to be a single, sixteen-year-old father. Which are things that I can't readily experience but that I'm able to experience through reading. Writing allowed me to learn so much about myself and to affirm that sense of self. So I think those tools are the most valuable ones that I have in my personal toolkit. And probably the most valuable ones that someone in general could have in their toolkit. I think of the library as the great equalizer. For me, for so long, I couldn't afford to buy books. But it didn't mean that I couldn't access exposure. I think that continues to be one of the great services of the library. It provides communities with all sorts of educational events and resources that are sometimes overwhelming.

MQPress: How have you used libraries for your latest work?

Molinary: Yesterday I gave a speech for a summer reading celebration to promote literacy at a high school in South Carolina. And they had a range of book to read over the summer. And I used the library to access the books and get them read. So I could know where they were coming from and what stories they had in their heads. So it helped me to come prepared for a relevant conversation with young adults because I don't often read young adult fiction now. So it was a quick way to access those books.

George Norfleet

McQueen Press

D.C. resident, Norfleet, is a graduate of Hampton University. *A Pilot's Journey: Memoirs of a Tuskegee Airman, Curtis Christopher Robinson* (Robnor Publishing) is his first book. Norfleet's effort reveals the reasons Tuskegee Airmen decided to fly and why they prevailed with other challenges throughout their lives. *A Pilot's Journey* is available at the Smithsonian Air and Space Museum, the National Archives in Washington, D.C., and at Robnor.

Interview at American Library Association Summer Meeting. Washington, DC. 2007

MQPress: Please describe your earliest experience as a library user, visitor, patron, or customer.

Norfleet: I recall my earliest library use as a child. I grew up in a rural area so mostly it was the libraries that we had at our school. But as I got to be, probably in the third or fourth grade, I used to check out books from the bookmobile. And that was a source of entertainment to us for the summertime because in a rural area, there can be very little to do. So I was quite fond of checking out books from the bookmobile and it was a way for me to entertain myself.

MQPress: How did libraries contribute to your early career as a writer?

Norfleet: I think libraries contributed to my desire to read and to acquire knowledge. I'm not sure that I can say definitively my experience with the library was anything that led me to writing. But it certainly developed my love for reading and learning. I guess that's the other half of the coin of being a writer.

MQPress: What types of reading materials or books are in your personal book collection or library?

Norfleet: All types of books. I'm a big fan of Afro-American history. We have a lot of books about the Tuskegee Airmen.[57] I have Tiger Woods

---

[57] The Tuskegee Airmen was the name of a group of African American pilots who flew during World War II as the 332nd Fighter Group of the US Army Air Corps.

books. *The DaVinci Code*. Basically history books. A few things on dinosaurs and things of that sort. But I like history and science books as much as anything.

MQPress: Besides libraries what other resources do you use to research your writing?

Norfleet: Personal interviews of people familiar with the subject area. And the Internet has been a wealth of information about the research and background material on writing. So that has been the only other source. Personal interviews and a lot of research on the Internet.

MQPress: What value do you believe libraries have to the general public?

Norfleet: I think libraries have the value of spreading knowledge. I think the fact that libraries are a repository of such a vast amount of knowledge that you are able to draw from at no cost is hugely beneficial. I can only imagine what life must have been like many years ago before there were books or before there were libraries. My concern is that libraries are not playing as prominent role today with the computer and the Internet as it once did. But I think they are invaluable to a civilized and learned society.

MQPress: How have you used libraries for your latest work?

Norfleet: What we have done, basically, is use libraries as a means of distributing and selling books. We have had discussions with library groups in northern Virginia and Washington D.C. of late. I also use it as a resource to tie in to libraries around the nation. Regional library systems and things of that sort. But that's been basically it.

♩   ♩   ♩   ♩   ♩   ♩   ♩   ♩   ♩   ♩   ♩   ♩   ♩   ♩

Roscoe Orman

McQueen Press

Roscoe Orman has a four-decade acting career that includes the role of "Gordon Robinson" on *Sesame Street*. Theater credits include *Whose Got His Own, We Righteous Bombers,* and *The Fabulous Miss Marie.* He helped to found Harlem's New Lafayette Theater and worked with American Place Theater, Negro Ensemble Company, New York Shakespeare Festival. Author of *Sesame Street Dad: Evolution of an Actor,* lately, he has written and illustrated *Ricky and Mobo* for Inkwater Press.

Interview at American Library Association Mid-Winter Meeting. Seattle, WA. 2007

MQPress: Please describe your earliest experience as a library user, visitor, patron, or customer.

Orman: I'm a native of Bronx, New York. In my early years of school, and even prior to school, my grandmother, in particular, would introduce me to our local library in the Bronx. I got my library card when I was very young. I just remember the magic and the wonder of going to the library with her. And experiencing books and the ability to actually take them home and read them. It just began what has become a lifelong fascination with books.

MQPress: How did libraries contribute to your early career as a writer?

Orman: Being an avid reader throughout school and a user of libraries as a resource just for enjoyment, I also used it naturally as a resource for my early writings as a poet. I'm a great fan of so many poets. Particularly African American poetry - Langston Hughes, Paul Laurence Dunbar. So libraries were my initial source of being exposed to those writers. And then in my own recent writings, my memoir and my children's book which is due out this year. I've continued to be inspired by books that I've read. Many of which were introduced [to me] by the libraries that I used.

MQPress: What types of reading materials or books are in your own personal book collection or library?

Orman: I like to read all kinds of books. I go through phases, actually. There are periods in which I tried to read as much fiction as possible. I just love the imagination and sense of style that is possible from great writers of fiction. But I'm currently reading more non-fiction. I guess from having written my own memoir I [was led in the direction of wanting] to see what other people are writing in terms of biography, history, and so forth. My own first book was not just my own personal history but also I expounded upon some of experiences that I had in the development of Black theater and children's television. That look at historical information is very important and as a father of four children I've got all kinds of books in my home for all different ages. So I enjoy quite a range of topics.

MQPress: Besides libraries what other resources do you use to research your writing?

Orman: Besides libraries. Well, as I said, I have a lot of books in my own personal collection. I also rely a lot upon my own observation of people and events. Just talking to people trying to get insight into whatever topics that I'm interested in. From my years and decades of work as an actor, I've developed an ability to study people in a way that is really important for my craft as an actor and performer. I hope to use some of those same skills to develop my awareness and knowledge for writing in terms of really using resources from direct interaction with as wide a range of people as possible.

MQPress: What value do you believe libraries have to the general public?

Orman: I think public libraries throughout our nation and many, many communities in this country are one of the greatest resources that we have as a people. For all ages. For children, obviously, to be able to go to the library for reference, for schoolwork, or just for enjoyment and develop a love for books and reading is so essential. And as we go through our lives just knowing that we have books accessible to us free of charge by being members of our local libraries is a wonderful gift. I think of it akin to public broadcasting, public television, and public radio[58] and other resources that we have that are so valuable to our

---

[58] Public broadcasting is a form of public service intended to serve the needs of the public. Radio, television, and other electronic media outlets receive some or all of their funding from the public. Broadcaster funds come either directly from individuals through donations and license fees, or indirectly as state subsidies raised from taxes. Many public broadcasters supplement these funds with sales of materials relevant to broadcasts as well as contributions from corporations, in return for underwriting.

education and identification as humans. I can't imagine not having libraries available to us.

MQPress: How have you used libraries for your latest work?

Orman: The children's book that I've completed and is set for release soon is something that comes from my own personal experience. So really I didn't really have a lot of direct need for other resources for that particular project. I am beginning the early stages of my next book for adults which deals with Black father hood – African American father figures. It's something that I'm beginning to research through various publications in the libraries. Online as well. I do a lot of research on the Internet. It's just good to know that that kind of wealth of resource information is available both online and in the libraries.

Jeff Savage

McQueen Press

Jeff Savage is a leading author of non-fiction children's books. With more than 150 books (*Tiger Woods, LeBron James, Danica Patrick, etc.*) in print, his biographies include role models of sports and entertainment, current events, and history as school curriculum. He won the International Reading Association's Children's Choice Award eight times as well as the Voice of Youth Advocates Non-Fiction Honor Award.

Interview at American Library Association Summer Meeting. Washington, DC. 2007

MQPress: Please describe your earliest experience as a library user, visitor, patron, or customer.

Savage: In my elementary library in third grade, as I recall, it was 1968. I remember the first book I checked out was a book on a baseball player named Babe Ruth. And I read the book and I finished the book and I checked out another book on a baseball player named Lou Gehrig. There were only two baseball books, two sports books in my elementary school. So I checked them out over and over. That's my earliest experience. Checking out those same two books over and over again. I was very grateful to have those two books.

MQPress: How did libraries contribute to your early career as a writer?

Savage: The writing part of it? I really wasn't much of a writer. I was more of a math guy. They pretty much did everything for me. They pretty much did everything for me. They did everything. Probably about 97.6% important. The other 2.4% was when I wrote. The 97.6% was when I did my research. The research is the critical part of writing. Because if you want to write well you have to do research. You have to learn all the information. Especially me because I write non-fiction.

MQPress: What types of reading materials or books are in your personal book collection or library?

Savage: I have too many to even count. What types of reading materials? I've written 174 books so I have 174 of my own books in my personal library. Plus my son's library which is down the hall from the office. My son has 174. I have to save copies for them. Those are my wife's orders. My favorite book of all time – I'm not that religious so I couldn't say the Bible because I wouldn't say that just to say it because I'm not super-religious - is the dictionary. My second favorite is the thesaurus. Those two books, the thesaurus and the dictionary sit next to my desk in my office. All kinds of books. Just research books. I like research. I'm a research type of guy.

MQPress: Besides libraries what other resources do you use to research your writing?

Savage: Okay, the first thing I use is the Internet. I go on the World Wide Web, as we call it, and do my preliminary research there. But I don't rely on any of the information I find on the Internet because a lot of it's unreliable. What I write has to be accurate. There could be no factual misinformation. I write non-fiction books for students ages probably… seven to sixteen, seventeen, eighteen, around there. A lot of high school students read my books. Reluctant readers. Usually, I write for a third to eighth grade reading level. I have to be careful and make sure that everything I write is correct. So I use that as a preliminary but then I go to the library. That's where I get the bulk of my information. Like here, 174 pages of information on a guy named David Beckham. He's a soccer player. I will have to email my questions to him. Because he's a real popular guy. That's what his publicist said. Last month, I talked to Ryan Howard, a Philadelphia Phillies baseball player on the phone for about an hour. Before I talked to him, I talked to his mom. I talked to his dad. I did interviews with people who know the person. And that's another way I get information. And then I go to the game to meet the player, to meet the athlete that I have to write a book about. But again, the bulk of the information I get is from sources that I find in the library. Periodicals, newspapers, magazines. Maybe there might be another book written about the person. I don't necessarily trust what's written because I know how books are made because I make them. I trust more reliable sources like *Sports Illustrated* or *The Los Angeles Times* or *The New York Times*. Major metropolitan newspapers are more reliable. The bulk of my information comes from libraries and actual interviews with people.

MQPress: What value do you believe libraries have to the general public?

Savage: Immense value. How do I say this? There should be more money spent on libraries both public and school. For instance, a school librarian should be in every school in the country. I know entire school districts, entire counties that don't have librarians staffing elementary schools.[59] That's insane. Kids need to learn how to maneuver in libraries. It's mind-boggling how much they're underused. Everybody should have to serve two years in the library. Just like we used to have a military draft? There should be a two-year service requirement for all United States citizens to attend at least weekly sessions in the library to familiarize themselves with education and knowledge. That's my opinion. Libraries are useful, valuable.

MQPress: How have you used libraries for your latest work?

Savage: I do have my David Beckham 174 pages right here. I pretty much have a routine where I go into the library. Sometimes I go online and just print out stuff from a library that's about an hour from my house. I'm a member of that library so I have a card. So I just use Ebscohost,[60] as its called, and get information that way. But I often go into the libraries and talk to reference librarians. They're great. They're really cool. And they're super smart. I don't know people who are quiet all the time. Me, I talk all the time, so what does that say? Let's skip that. But I use them in every capacity that they can be utilized, I suspect. There are many facets of the library that I don't know. However, every month I seem to learn something new at a library. So I should never assume that I know all. Yeah, I use libraries pretty much in every capacity that they can be.

⌐ ⌐ ⌐ ⌐ ⌐ ⌐ ⌐ ⌐ ⌐ ⌐ ⌐ ⌐ ⌐ ⌐ ⌐

---

[59] Excerpt from a letter addressed to the United States Congress from Representatives Raul Grijalva (D-AZ) and Vernon Ehlers (R-MI) dated August 1, 2007, "SUPPORT A HIGHLY QUALIFIED LIBRARIAN FOR EVERY SCHOOL, Cosponsor HR 2864, the Strengthening Kids' Interest in Learning and Libraries Act. Dear Colleague: Please join us in cosponsoring HR 2864, The Strengthening Kids' Interest in Learning and Libraries or SKILLs Act. This bill guarantees that students across America will be served by highly qualified, state-certified school library media specialists and the library resources they need to succeed. Study after study proves that students in schools with well-stocked libraries and highly qualified, state-certified school librarians learn more, get better grades and score higher on standardized tests than students who do not have the same benefits. **Today, only 60 percent of school libraries have full-time, state-certified school library media specialists on staff.** With limited resources, school administrators are struggling to stretch dollars, and library resource budgets are increasingly being used to make up for shortfalls in other areas…"

[60] Excerpt from Ebsco Publishing's website, "EBSCO Publishing is the home of EBSCOhost, the world's leading Internet research service. The technology behind EBSCOhost powers databases that provide researchers around the globe with information."

Dackeyia Q. Sterling

McQueen Press

Sterling is a former Hollywood literary agent and talent manager. With fifteen years of industry experience and education from Howard University, she is now the CEO/Publisher of *Entertainment Power Players*, a ready reference directory of contacts for people who work or desire to work in the entertainment industry. Some categories used by jobseekers, film festival organizers, producers include "Writing Workshops" as well as "Animation Companies."

Interview at American Library Association Summer Meeting. Washington, DC. 2007

MQPress: Please describe your earliest experience as a library user, visitor, patron, or customer.

Sterling: I remember going to the library on a field trip in elementary school as a visitor and just seeing all these books was amazing. But in fifth grade, I specifically remember being excused from class because our teacher was teaching evolution.[61] And I didn't believe in evolution. I raised my hand and said, "Ms. Jensen, I don't believe in evolution." So she sent me to the library every day while she taught evolution. While I was there, I discovered a book on Phyllis Wheatley. That was the first one. And then Martin Luther King and then Rosa Parks. And then I was done. I was in heaven. The world opened up to me. I read those poems and those odes that Phyllis Wheatley that wrote and I was like, "Oh my gosh!" I just had a connection in my heart and in my spirit with the books.

MQPress: How did libraries contribute to your early career as a writer?

---

[61] The scientific theory of evolution maintains that all living things descend from a single common ancestor. The creation vs. evolution debate, or the origins debate, or the evolution controversy disputes the origins of the Earth, humanity, life, and the universe. This debate triggers considerable discussion in view of public school education regarding which theory, Creationism or Evolution, should be taught to students.

Sterling: I think it fostered a love for writing and an appreciation for English. An appreciation for words. An appreciation for the physical texture of books. So now I'm publisher. I appreciate the quality of books now.

MQPress: What types of reading materials or books are in your personal book collection or library?

Sterling: I have a lot of autobiographies. I love reading about people's life stories. I have a lot of self-help books. A lot of Bibles and spiritually-based materials. And a lot of magazines.

MQPress: Besides libraries what other resources do you use to research your writing?

Sterling: I do conferences. I use the Internet. I talk to people. I do a lot of interviews.

MQPress: What value do you believe libraries have to the general public?

Sterling: I think libraries are priceless. I think you can learn anything in the universe at the library. I think you can be inspired for a lifetime by visiting the library. I think you that can meet people. You can understand the world in which we live a lot better by visiting libraries.

MQPress: How have you used libraries for your latest work?

Sterling: The latest work is called *Entertainment Power Players*. It's a [television], film, music, and sports directory. This directory is a compilation of those industries, those genres. So I didn't really use the library that much. For the first edition we did. I would say just researching those industries and understanding them a lot better I did use the library. A little bit.

♩ ♩ ♩ ♩ ♩ ♩ ♩ ♩ ♩ ♩ ♩ ♩ ♩ ♩ ♩

Chapter 6

Academic, Technical & Professional Writers

Academy – Institution of higher education or the faculty of an institution of higher education. A body of learned people. Various associations of scholars, artists, literary men and women, and scientists, organized for the promotion of general or special intellectual or artistic interests, not necessarily connected with any distinct school.

Technical – Having special knowledge of a subject, particularly mechanical or scientific. Relating to a particular practical or scientific subject or mode of training.

Technology – Applied science. A technical method of achieving a practical purpose.

Profession - Certain types of skilled work at a recognized standard of ability requiring formal training, or extensive academic study. Professions control the training, evaluation, licensing, certification, ethics, procedures, protocols, and admission of members. Members of professions exercise independent judgement and ethics. Often the required skill sets of a profession are rewarded by payment or salary.

Mohammed Aman

McQueen Press

Born in Alexandria, Egypt, Aman studied at Cairo, Columbia, and Pittsburgh universities. On faculty of the School of Information Science at University of Wisconsin – Milwaukee, he is editor of *Domes (Digest of Middle Eastern Studies)*, a journal that discusses Middle East issues. He has also authored, co-authored, or edited works such as *Cataloging and Classification of Non-Western Library Materials*, *The New Bibliotheca Alexandria*, *Librarianship and the Third World.*

Interview at American Library Association Summer Meeting. Washington, DC. 2007

MQPress: Please describe your earliest experience as a library user, visitor, patron, or customer.

Aman: My first experience was probably when I was about fourteen or fifteen years old. I grew up in a country like Egypt where, at the time, in the 1950s, it didn't have public libraries as such.[62] So the library I went to was actually called a circulation library or renting library. You rented a book. So I had to pay money to get the book and read it as fast as I could in order to go back and get the other book. And so on and so forth. It was similar in America in the 1700s to a subscription library.[63] You subscribed and therefore, you had to really read as fast as you could to make your money go a long way. At the time I read biographies, history and translations. The literature of Tolstoy, *War and Peace*, as well as Hemingway, and many of the literature that was available at the time in these libraries.

MQPress: How did libraries contribute to your early career as a writer?

---

[62] This is likely the best place to note that The Royal Library of Alexandria, Egypt during the reign of Ptolemy II circa 300 B.C., was the largest library in the world at that time. Though diminished by war and fire by 800 A.D., at its height, the Royal Library actively gathered Hellenistic manuscripts and served a wide geography of Mediterranean and Eastern empires.

[63] Subscription library [see Glossary of Library Terms].

Aman: I think without it I wouldn't be here in my position as a professor and as a writer. I was what you consider today, a bookworm. In fact, my mother used to really feel upset. Everyone was going to the beach and playing. I think at one point she thought there was something wrong with her son. I remember her saying, "Mohammed, why don't you go to the beach and play with the kids and go swimming?" And I would say, "I'm really happy sitting here reading my book." My mother was illiterate. She thought her son was really anti-social or whatever. It turned out that I was a very fine person. The books contributed to my being even a better person. Because of that, I decided to go the Faculty of Arts at Cairo University which is really the most prestigious university. I went to the English Department first. Most of the books I read were translated from English. I left English and went to the Library Science Department at Cairo University. Then the rest is history. I got a scholarship to go to Columbia University for my Master's and then the University of Pittsburgh for my Ph.D. I continued to read and write and really be a librarian.

MQPress: What types of reading materials or books are in your personal book collection or library?

Aman: Mostly, international literature as well as biography, history, politics. I am not really what is considered a fan of fiction. Some of them I will read. My wife is a fiction writer. She loves science fiction. My son is a science fiction reader. But I tend more toward these subjects I have mentioned. Now and then she would say, "Oh, you should read that book." So I read the book by [Khaled Hosseini] which is *The Kite Runner* which is going to be made into a movie as we speak. That was fascinating because it is a combination of autobiography, history, and fiction dealing with Afghanistan. Literature, but not really the fiction that people really read. Science fiction is not my forte but the ones I have mentioned are.

MQPress: Besides libraries what other resources do you use to research your writing?

Aman: Nowadays, the Internet. When I came along in that field, the only thing was really the written word which was the book. Nobody ever imagined that we would have, even my professors at Columbia University, Columbia University, ha! you will never see a reference book online. Guess what? We have everything now online. I think really navigating the Internet in search of full-text reference books, articles, even fiction books. Isaac Asimov, for example, was able to write even more books when they gave him a computer. They had to convince him.[64] I'm sure if Ernest Hemingway were alive and he had a computer, he would have multiplied his writing. All of a sudden, the Internet has really opened a huge world for us. Much to the dismay of those who said one or the other, well, guess what? We are really enjoying both the printed book as well as the Internet. The two really complement one another. I studied information science when I went to the University of Pittsburgh They think that I was really, really ancient because we were dealing with punch cards, paper tapes. We had to do our own programming. Nowadays, my gosh, everything is done for you. It's a fascinating world, a fascinating time. My son has his Palm[65] and he puts all his books he wants to read on his Palm. When he's on the plane, he reads it. He taught his mother how to use it. She now has the books on her Palm. So she doesn't have to lug the big paperbacks although she still does.

MQPress: What value do you believe libraries have to the general public?

Aman: Libraries are really our life blood, frankly. They are essential tools not only to democracy but to entertainment, for joy, for employment. I feel sorry for people who really don't have that luxury because I went through that as a young man growing in an impoverished country like in Egypt where there was no such thing as public libraries to go to. You either [had to] know somebody or there were the subscription libraries. Even when they had public libraries the books were too old or in bad shape. The librarian's considered to be the custodian. Meaning that if he loses a book, it is cut from his salary and his pension. So it wasn't to his advantage to really circulate books in the library. I think those who are unfortunately deprived of libraries around the world are really deprived of their essential freedom. To me, libraries are that kind of freedom where you can really go and dream, explore the world. Learn about the other side of the world. All of these things. I'm here, for example,

---

[64] Isaac Asimov (1920-1992) was a well-known science fiction writer. For the majority of Asimov's writing career, word processing and personal computers were not common to the general public. Word processing developed in the 1970s and became more accessible to personal computers during the 1980s. By Asimov's death in 1992, the possibilities of word-processing became more well-known. Still famously prolific, Asimov has approximately 515 books in his bibliography (either as author or editor) in nine of ten Dewey Decimal System ranges (the exception being Philosophy).

[65] A Palm is a type of personal digital assistant. PDAs are handheld computers originally designed as personal organizers. However, PDAs are also used for clocks, calendars, address books, emails, web browsers, video recording, word processing, spreadsheet calculation, bar code scans, mobile phones, media players, computer games, and Global Positioning System (GPS).

collecting books for Africa. Because there are many African libraries that don't have the money to buy books. So as a result I collect them and send them. In fact, the cultural attaché from the Tanzanian Embassy is coming here Tuesday to pick up the picks I'm donating. I'm hoping that other publishers will donate and send them in boxes to other libraries in Tanzania and Kenya.

MQPress: How have you used libraries for your latest work?

Aman: Every write I have to explore. The first thing you start with is the idea. After the idea, you start searching for the material. You start really going through indexes. Search for keywords. Then gather the background. So its very much like the literature search that you learn from scholarship. Then, of course, identify what's available in libraries and on the Internet. Gather all that material to start reading and researching and then, of course, you start your writing. You are hoping, of course, to expand on what others have written. To really write your own experience. That I find very important especially when I edit my journal, *Digest of Middle Eastern Studies*. Either when I'm editing articles sent to me by scholars or when I'm writing reviews of books that will have to be published in my journal.

⌐ ⌐ ⌐ ⌐ ⌐ ⌐ ⌐ ⌐ ⌐ ⌐ ⌐ ⌐ ⌐ ⌐ ⌐

John Burgess

John Burgess is an engineer, educator, and entrepreneur. He has worked as a high tech product engineer and manager in the Silicon Valley. He's also worked as a business broker, business owner, Internet company executive, and product import company executive. Currently, he works with A+ School Tech Tools LLC to find and share education technology tools that increase student performance. His writing centers primarily on business and technology efforts.

McQueen Press

Interview at American Library Association Mid-Winter Meeting. Seattle, WA. 2007

MQPress: Please describe your earliest experience as a library user, visitor, patron, or customer.

Burgess: My earliest experience at going to the library was with my mother when I was probably two or three years old. My mother was a voracious reader. She would take me to the library. I don't know how often we would go, but it was a lot. I would spend time in the children's section. By the second or third grade I ventured into the adult section and picked out my own books. I remember picking out, when I was in the third grade, a huge 800-page book on yoga. I remember arguing with my mother whether or not it was something I would be able to get anything out of. She let me check it out. The library just really inspired my thinking at a very young age. To be able to go there and see all the different books and looking through them. Having that model by my mother who's always been a very avid reader.

MQPress: How did libraries contribute to your early career as a writer?

Burgess: Well, obviously, in order to get ideas for writing, you have to do a lot of reading. Especially when I was in college, I went to the libraries a lot. Sometimes I would go there for specific purposes to look at particular books. But a lot of times, when I was done with my own research I would look around the tables at books left by other people. I would pick those books up on subjects that I probably had no business reading. I went to UC Davis. I can remember reading some at UC Davis

Chapter 6 – Academic, Technical & Professional Writers 119

in the engineering library, seeing books on medical engineering. Getting ideas on those as well. Being in the library was just incredibly important to inspire the thinking and get the knowledge that is required to put together something that's interesting for other people.

MQPress: What types of reading materials or books are in your personal book collection or library?

Burgess: Well, I kind of started with the books from college. When I was in college, I saved all my books. I was a bibliophile.[66] Is that the right word? I have all of my text books. I was in college the first time for seven years. The first three years I was there, I took every subject under the sun. It was a four year program. I have all my books from all of those different classes. I used to go to book fairs and library sales. I would go through the stacks and buy books. I used to read seven or eight books at a time. I wasn't the kind of person who could read books serially. I'd read as much as I could, then I put it to the bottom and go to the next pile and I'd pick up the next book and go through these eight books. I kept a lot of those books. I've gotten books from friends over the years. My house is littered with books. I've got boxes of books. I've got closets filled with books. I've got bookshelves. There are books all over the place.

MQPress: Besides libraries, what other resources do you use to research your writing?

Burgess: Well now I primarily use the Internet. The resources and search tools are just so incredibly good now. You can almost become an expert in a short period of time on just about any subject if you have the proper background. One of the reasons I became an engineer in the first place was because someone told me with an engineering background you can think about just about anything. I found that to be largely true. Especially in this technological age that we live in. Right now, mainly, most of the research that I do is online. I have another business that is related to the natural foods industry and I needed to become an expert in natural foods and health. So I went online. I used a lot of resources, for instance, with the National Institutes of Health website. I was able to read scientific literature which wasn't available ten or fifteen years ago. I wouldn't have been able to access that kind of information. I made myself an expert in that field. Right now we're in the business of education technology. One of the products that we sell is reading software. So I'm becoming an expert in the science of reading. A lot of

---

[66] Bibliophile [see Glossary of Library Terms].

that information has come from either other authors that I know or the Internet research that I do.

MQPress: How have you used libraries for your latest work?

Burgess: I really haven't used libraries that much at all. It seems like libraries are still clinging to some old models which require they have books in the stacks. They're becoming less useful for me. If they could rethink their business model and think of themselves more as people who are resources for finding information through all means through their own collections or through the Internet or various other means, I think I would probably use them more. As it is, right now, I can do a Google search and come up with relevant up-to-the-minute things that they probably wouldn't have in their own collections.

♩   ♩   ♩   ♩   ♩   ♩   ♩   ♩   ♩   ♩   ♩   ♩   ♩   ♩   ♩

Anthony Hodge

Having worked in the Phoenix Public Library system, Hodge brings a practical background to the logistics of library software. He is Marketing and Communications Manger of Medialab Solutions BV in Amsterdam, The Netherlands which developed *AquaBrowser Online*, a search tool and digital resource aggregator. He co-wrote *Risen: Why Libraries are Here to Stay* to discuss the library's role in a world of emerging technology.

McQueen Press

Interview at American Library Association Summer Meeting. Washington, DC. 2007

MQPress: Please describe your earliest experience as a library user, visitor, patron, or customer.

Hodge: The earliest experience I remember is probably third grade with the school librarian and getting to learn the library card catalog, of course. How to use the card catalog. As a later library patron, probably in high school and university, the difference for me was while was studying at the university, I actually started working at the library. So I was a library page and, of course, user because I did all my studying and homework at the library. I'm from Phoenix so I became very familiar with the Phoenix Public Library collection at the main branch but also the entire system - the other branches around the city. From there, I became a library assistant then started doing reference and had my own desk. Most of my experience using the library was on both sides both doing reference for other people and doing my own research while I was attending university.

MQPress: How did libraries contribute to your early career as a writer?

Hodge: I would say that academically, most of my writing was research-based for my study. The library was where I went for all of my information. I'm thirty now, so I'm in the generation that was just, I'd say, pre-Internet. When I had to do research, I did everything myself. I used the library catalog. There was no Google in the day that I was finishing my degree. Information I was able to put my hands on was library-based. It was all verified information.[67] I'm not saying that what's on the Internet is all unverified, but there's a lot of stuff that isn't on there. As a writer, the book that I wrote is about libraries. It's about working in the library and what libraries need. Obviously, the library *(unintelligible)* my entire subject.

MQPress: What types of reading materials or books are in your personal book collection or library?

Hodge: My first degree was in political science. My second degree was in European public affairs. I'm very interested in humor and politics. I'd say, in my personal collection, I only buy books that I like to read personally. I don't like to buy books that I use for work. My personal collection is filled with political science satire.

MQPress: Besides libraries what other resources do you use to research your writing?

Hodge: Obviously, I do use the Internet, so I do web searches. I will try to find authors of journals or articles in journals. I like to try to speak to the authors directly. I usually cite them as a resource if I can speak to the horse's mouth, so to speak.

MQPress: What value do you believe libraries have to the general public?

Hodge: I think libraries are invaluable to the general public. I wrote the book, *Risen: Why Libraries are Here to Stay*, because I believe that libraries are here to stay. For me, the library is the central information point of every community. I think that libraries sort of need to retake that role. They've always been in that role it's just that the community doesn't necessarily see them that way. I think library patronage maybe is not what it used to be because there are other places, more convenient places, online places where you can get your information. More and more libraries are online and you can go to their catalog just as easily as you can go perform a web search. I feel that the content the library can provide is verified. It's collected by professionals. It's also neutral. It's the most objective information that you can get your hands on. And that's why the library will always remain the most relevant to its community.

MQPress: How have you used libraries for your latest work?

Hodge: As I said, libraries are the topic of the book that I've written. I use many examples. Different cities. Specifically, the public library in Amsterdam was a great example because they're very progressive in their thinking and in the image they want to build in their city. They want to

---

[67] Scholarly resources [see Glossary of Library Terms].

be viewed as hip as the latest club that's great in Amsterdam. That's one city. That's the way that that city is catering to its patronage. Another city library might be Chicago where they're a bit more conservative. They would much more be reflected upon as perhaps the library that contains all information in the entire region and really cater to its very mixed population, very broad population, rather than specifics.

⌐ ⌐ ⌐ ⌐ ⌐ ⌐ ⌐ ⌐ ⌐ ⌐ ⌐ ⌐ ⌐ ⌐ ⌐

Olofunmilayo Olopade

David Christopher

Professor at the University of Chicago's Department of Medicine, Olopade holds the MacArthur "Genius" Grant. She is Director of the Center for Clinical Cancer Research. She researches genetics of breast cancer, risk and prevention, hematology and oncology. She co-authored *Breast Cancer in Women of African Descent* and wrote articles for *National Institutes of Health, JAMA, New England Journal of Medicine, Radiology*, and *Cancer Research*, among many others.

Interview at Blacks in Science Program. Loyola University. Chicago, IL. 2007

MQPress: Please describe your earliest experience as a library user, visitor, patron, or customer.

Olopade: That would have to be in my high school library where I went to look for a book to do a research paper in physics. Finding the literature to back the experiment I wanted to do. I remember that the book was expensive so I couldn't afford it so I had to use the library's copy.

MQPress: How did libraries contribute to your early career as a writer?

Olopade: Well so, I do scientific writing. There are a lot of papers you want to cite. You want to also review the literature to make sure you're covering things that you may think that no one's already thought about. But it's already in the archives. So it's been very valuable and very important to be able to go to a reference library and look at the collections and things that people wrote a hundred years ago. But if you have a good library, they might be able to get you archival material. We've also used the library to look for things I've studied with microfilm. It's been very helpful for me.

MQPress: What types of reading materials or books are in your personal book collection or library?

Olopade: Well so, one of the things that really hurt scientists is that you spend so much time doing science you don't have time to enjoy reading for fun. I have a daughter who's a literature major. So my house is filled with books. I buy books for my children. So as a busy scientist, even though I don't read as much as I should. I actually have a huge collection of books from what my children have read and what I have bought for them in my house. My son, who is now seventeen, probably has every science fiction book ever published from Adams to Terry Pratchett. I grew up reading an English author called Eddie Blighton. So I think I have all her books. Alice Walker, other authors. We just buy books. We love books in our house. My father loved books so I grew up reading books. So I know that a good library is very important in the nurturing of children. So yes, my house has a very nice book collection.

MQPress: Besides libraries, what other resources do you use to research your writing?

Olopade: Well now, we're in the Internet age and so it's really easy to get information on the Internet. So I do use the Internet.

MQPress: What value do you believe the library has for the general public?

Olopade: Oh, a lot. Especially in Chicago the public library has really served our family very well. We have a library in Hyde Park on Blackstone. For many summers, that was sort of where we went to cool off. The Harold Washington Library is awesome. There are many books there. As my husband would say, you don't have to buy every book. You can go to the library and borrow a book. We use the library a lot. We borrow books from the library. It's great.

MQPress: How have you used libraries for your latest work?

Olopade: As I said, our field is rapidly evolving. What's most important now in terms of a science writer what we do is to be able to go to old literature to see the work that has been done. A lot of the new literature is on the Internet. You can easily access PDF[68] formats from your computer. But if you really want to look at the literature that was published even ten years ago, twenty years ago, which is really valuable, you have to be able to go to the library.

⌐ ⌐ ⌐ ⌐ ⌐ ⌐ ⌐ ⌐ ⌐ ⌐ ⌐ ⌐ ⌐

---

[68] Portable Document Format (PDF) is the file format created by Adobe Systems in 1993 for the exchange of documents with fixed layout that may include text, fonts, images, and graphics.

Chris Pramas

McQueen Press

Chris Pramas has worked with game lines such as *Warhammer Fantasy Roleplay, Feng Shui* and *Underground* and has been Creative Director for Miniatures at Wizards of the Coast. He founded Green Ronin Publishing, named Best Publisher by the GenCon & EnWorld Awards three years in a row. Author of the *AD&D Guide to Hell, Dragon Fist,* and *Death in Freeport,* he won three Origins and two ENnie Awards. *Hobby Games: the 100 Best* is the latest project.

Interview at American Library Association Mid-Winter Meeting. Seattle, WA. 2007

MQPress: Please describe your earliest experience as a library user visitor, patron, or customer.

Pramas: I grew up in a town called Peabody, Massachusetts. I used to go down to the local branch of the library system where I checked out my first science fiction books. That became a big influence on me later in life. And then as I got a little older I started going to the main branch of the library. We actually used to go there to not only check out books and things but also to play games. And so, it was at that library where I first started to play role-playing games[69] which I later turned into a career in designing games. So, libraries actually had a pretty formative effect on me as a writer and game designer.

MQPress: How did libraries contribute to your early career as a writer?

Pramas: So they gave me a place to play, as I mentioned. But also, things I've always been interested in have been historical in nature. I studied history in college so it was a great place to do research and find out about historical periods that I didn't have books on.

MQPress: What types of reading materials or books are in your personal book collection or library?

---

[69] Role-playing games require participants to assume the roles of fictional characters and collaboratively create or follow stories based on traits of those characters within a system of rules and guidelines. Computer role-playing game are a video game genre.

Pramas: Well, because I'm a game designer, I have lots of games for starters. The rest of my stuff is heavily skewed towards history books because I love history. And then a certain amount of genre fiction like fantasy and science fiction novels.

MQPress: Besides libraries, what other resources do you use to research your writing?

Pramas: Well, these days, it's the Internet. It's very handy when I'm in the office. If I need to look up something very quickly, a quick Google search will get basic info. Then I can follow up through other sources.

MQPress: What value do you believe libraries have to the general public?

Pramas: They have all sorts of value. One as centers of knowledge. No one can have as many books in their personal collection as a library. It's a great place to find out about topics that interest you. I think generally serving public education is a great thing that libraries do. They can also bring people together through programming. Maybe some young kids today will start playing games in libraries like I did and be the game designers of tomorrow.

MQPress: How have you used libraries for your latest work?

Pramas: My latest work is purely fictional. So I haven't used libraries for it. I did recently design a historical-based game though called *V for Victory*. I did use the library for that to piece out some of the more obscure references that I was looking for.

♩   ♩   ♩   ♩   ♩   ♩   ♩   ♩   ♩   ♩   ♩   ♩   ♩   ♩   ♩

Chapter 7

Classic Quotes

Writers have some pretty interesting thoughts and ideas about the role of libraries in their world. Some opinions are full of praise, others rather amused, some mocking, and some shocking.

Then and now, at the very least, writers were and are not indifferent to libraries which should bode well for the future of both.

Old School

"There are times when I think the ideal library is composed solely of reference books. They are like understanding friends; always ready to meet your mood, always ready to change the subject when you have had enough of this or that."
J. Donald Adams (*NY Times*)

"The richest minds need not libraries."
Amos Bronson Alcott (*Table Talk: Learning Books*)

"Libraries, which are as the shrines where all the relics of the ancient saints, full of true virtue, and that without delusion or imposture, are preserved and reposed."
Francis Bacon

"Books are not made for furniture, but there is nothing else that so beautifully furnishes a house."
Henry Ward Beecher

"A library is but the soul's burial-ground. It is the land of shadows."
Henry Ward Beecher (*Star Papers: Oxford: The Bodleian Library*)

"Libraries are not made, they grow."
"Good as it is to inherit a library, it is better to collect one."
Augustine Birrell (*Obiter Dicta. Book Buying*)

"I have always imagined that Paradise will be a kind of library."
Jorge Luis Borges

"The true University of these days is a collection of books."
Thomas Carlyle

"These are the tombs of such as cannot die."
George Crabbe (*The Library*)

"Real bibliophiles do not put their books on shelves for people to look at or handle. They have no desire to show off their darlings, or to amaze people with their possessions. They keep their prized books hidden away in a secret spot to which they resort stealthily, like a Caliph visiting his harem, or a church elder sneaking into a bar. To be a book collector is to combine the worst characteristics of a dope-fiend with those of a miser."
Robertson Davies

"A great library contains the diary of the human race."
Rev. George Dawson (*Address on Opening the Birmingham Free Library*)

"Don't join the book burners. Don't think you're going to conceal faults by concealing evidence that they ever existed. Don't be afraid to go in your library and read every book."
Dwight D. Eisenhower

"It is not observed that… librarians are wiser men than others."
Ralph Waldo Emerson

"Meek young men grow up in libraries, believing it their duty to accept the views which Cicero, which Locke, which Bacon have given, forgetful that Cicero, Locke and Bacon were only young men in libraries when they wrote their books."
Ralph Waldo Emerson

"I know how busy you are in your library, which is your Paradise."
Desiderius Erasmus (*Letter to Bishop Fisher*)

"Such libraries had made common tradesmen and farmers as intelligent as gentlemen elsewhere and had contributed to the ability of Americans to defend their privileges."
Benjamin Franklin (*Autobiography*)

"It is vanity to persuade the world one hath much learning, by getting a great library."
Thomas Fuller (*Holy and Profane State: Of Books*)

"Twenty-two concubines, and a library of sixty-thousand volumes attested the variety of his inclinations; and from the productions which he left behind him, it appears that both the one and the other were designed for use rather than for ostentation."
Edward Gibbon (on Emperor Gordian the Younger)

"He that revels in a well-chosen library, has innumerable dishes, and all admirable flavour."
William Godwin (*The Enquirer: Early Taste for Reading*)

"Every library should try to be complete on something, if it were only the history of pinheads."
Oliver Wendell Holmes (*The Poet at the Breakfast Table*)

"I have often thought that nothing would do more extensive good at small expense than the establishment of a small circulating library in every county, to consist of a few well-chosen, to be lent to the people of the county, under such regulations as would secure their safe return in due time."
Thomas Jefferson (*Writings*)

"A man will turn over half a library to make one book."
Samuel Johnson (*Life of Johnson*)

"No place affords a more striking conviction of the vanity of human hopes than a public library."
Samuel Johnson

"Thou art the book-
The library whereon I look."
Henry King, Bishop of Chichester. (*Exequy on the Death of a Beloved Wife*)

"If I were founding a university I would found first a smoking room; then when I had a little more money in hand I would found a dormitory; then after that, or more probably with it, a decent reading room and a library. After that, if I still had more money that I couldn't use, I would hire a professor and get some textbooks."
Stephen Leacock (*Oxford As I See It*)

"Borrowers of books – those mutilators of collections, spoilers of the symmetry of shelves, and creators of odd volumes."
Charles Lamb (*Essays of Elia*, 'The Two Races of Men')

"Sir, the fact that a book is in a public library brings no comfort. Books are the one element in which I am personally and nakedly acquisitive. If it weren't for the law I would steal them. If it weren't for my purse, I would buy them."
Harold J. Laski (*Holmes-Laski Letters*)

"I find television very educational. The minute someone turns it on, I go to the library and read a good book."
Groucho Marx

"Affect not as some do that bookish ambition to be stored with books and have well furnished libraries, yet keep their heads empty of knowledge, to desire to have many books, and never to use them, is like a child that will have a candle burning by him all the while he is sleeping."
Henry Peacham (*The Compleat Gentleman*)

"What do we, as a nation, care about books? How much do you think we spend altogether on our libraries, public or private, as compared with what we spend on our horses?"
John Ruskin

"We call ourselves a rich nation, and we are filthy and foolish enough to thumb each other's books out of circulating libraries."
John Ruskin

"Knowing I lov'd my books, he furnished me.
From mine own library with volumes that
I prize above my dukedom."
William Shakespeare (*The Tempest*)

"Madam, a circulating library in town is as an evergreen tree of diabolical knowledge!"
Richard Brinsley Sheridan (*The Rivals*)

"For I bless God in the libraries of the learned and for all the booksellers in the world."
Christopher Smart (*Jubilate Agno fra*)

"People who want to understand democracy should spend less time in the library with Aristotle and more time on the buses and in the subway."
Simeon Strunsky (*No Mean City*)

"And further, by these, my son, be admonished: of making many books there is no end; and much study is a weariness of the flesh."
Unknown (*The Holy Bible: Ecclesiastes 12:12*)

"A person's library consists of all the books he has that no one wants to borrow."
Unknown

"Knowledge is free at the library. Just bring your own container."
Unknown

"A library is an arsenal of liberty."
Unknown

"Nutrimentum spiritus." Or "Food for the soul."
Unknown (Inscription on Berlin Royal Library)

"Medicine for the soul." Or "A sanatorium for the mind."
Unknown (Inscription on Library at Thebes, Alexandria, Egypt)

"Henceforth I whimper no more, post-pone no more, need nothing,
Done with indoor complaints, libraries, querulous criticisms,
Strong and content I travel the open road."
Walt Whitman (*Leaves of Grass. Song of the Open Road*)

"There is no such thing as a moral or immoral book. Books are either well written or badly written."
Oscar Wilde

"I read prodigiously. The Widener Library has crumpled under my attack. Ten, twelve, fifteen books a day are nothing."
Thomas Wolfe

"And I must read a little Ibsen to compare with Euripides – Racine with Sophocles – perhaps Marlowe with Aeschylus. Sounds very learned; but really might amuse me; and if it doesn't, no need to go on."
Virginia Woolfe (*A Writer's Diary*)

New School

"My earliest experience in the library was at Iowa State University. I took a one-credit course in library and library systems. I had to do a bibliography. I hated it. It was one of the hardest courses I had taken. But I was able to publish a book."
Zaid Abdul-Aziz (p. 83)

"I think those who are unfortunately deprived of libraries around the world are really deprived of their essential freedom."
Mohammed Aman (p. 117)

"Libraries are the heart and soul of any community. Even as we go more and more online for information, libraries still contain the solid stepping stones of civilization. Support your libraries; safeguard civilization."
Rudolfo Anaya (p. 11)

"So in the big picture, you cannot have a democracy without a well-educated and well-rounded citizenry. Libraries are the heart of that process."
Jeff Angus (p. 87)

"The library is essentially an inspiration."
Alan Axelrod (p. 89)

"But in the past when I've done research, I used the library as much as possible as a primary source area. I tried to get the original documents as they were put out by the person that created the document. So the library is a very important place for writers to go and do documentary research."
Timuel D. Black, Jr. (p. 93)

"Because at a library, one can check out who's publishing books on certain themes and who does the most beautiful or wonderful books of the sort one wants to do. And then one knows who to send their work to."
Claire Buchwald (p. 94)

"It seems like libraries are still clinging to some old models which require they have books in the stacks. They're becoming less useful for me. If they could rethink their business model and think of themselves more as people who are resources for finding information through all means through their own collections or through the Internet or various other means, I think I would probably use them more."
John Burgess (p. 121)

"The great thing about libraries is they're a great equalizer the same way public schools are equalizers."
Patrick Carman (p. 13)

"Especially at the larger libraries, they subscribe to a lot of databases. People go in and they use the databases sometimes even more than they'll look through the books in the stacks."
Anthony Chiffolo (p. 98)

"My orientation to the library was sort of like most people's. It was doing research for school projects. The first time it related to my work as a writer was when I was in a class that did one person shows. I was doing Nikki Giovanni. I remember doing some great research in the Northwestern University Library on Nikki Giovanni."
Lydia Diamond (p. 63)

"…Oh, I could walk any aisle
and smell wisdom, put a hand out to touch
the rough curve of bound leather,
the harsh parchment of dreams…"
Rita Dove (p. 39)
Excerpt from "Maple Valley Branch Library, 1967"

"So whatever you can find in your own life, including t.v. and movies and everything is great. But you can always count on the libraries to tell you about the past and the future and what people enjoy."
Cooper Edens (p. 15)

"At their most basic level, [libraries are] a warm, friendly place to get in out of the rain and find something to read."
Phil Foglio (p. 17)

"Eventually, they gave me special permission in the library to go and get adult books out from the adult section. I could only go in the science and non-fiction section. But I was a ten-year-old kid in the adult section of the library and it was pretty neat."
Dave Gegic (p. 41)

"I've always found librarians to be very helpful people. I think to the public they're a great resource. They are unique. It's a different experience than going to a book store."
Kirk Hanley (p. 67)

"It's the most objective information that you can get your hands on. And that's why the library will always remain the most relevant to its community."
Anthony Hodge (p. 123)

"I just don't foresee that libraries are ever going to go out of fashion."
J.A. Jance (p. 19)

"I think libraries are very, very important particularly in the United States when funding for arts – music and other sorts of arts and cultural activities - in public schools have been removed."
Quraysh Ali Lansana (p. 46)

"I think they are extremely important in educating the public about reading and books as well as teachers and parents."
Sheryl McFarlane (p. 21)

"The Internet is like having a library at your fingertips."
Anthony Ellis McGee (p. 23)

"I used the library as if it were my own expensive collection of books. Instead of me having the frame of mind where I had to own every book I like, I assume everything is in the library. I just let them hold my books for me."
Terry Moore (p. 24)

"The library was probably my greatest indulgence."
Rosie Molinary (p. 100)

"People need to understand the value of just reading. If we lose that, we are going to lose ourselves as a society."
John Nance (p. 29)

"They are the core to our culture. They are the beating heart. Libraries and library systems in this country are beating heart of our U.S., American culture. They are indispensable."
Raúl Niño (p. 49)

"I'm not sure that I can say definitively my experience with the library was anything that led me to writing. But it certainly developed my love for reading and learning. I guess that's the other half of the coin of being a writer."
George Norfleet (p. 103)

"What's most important now in terms of a science writer what we do is to be able to go to old literature to see the work that has been done. A lot of the new literature is on the Internet. You can easily access PDF formats from your computer. But if you really want to look at the literature that was published even ten years ago, twenty years ago, which is really valuable, you have to be able to go to the library."
Funmilayo Olopade (p. 126)

"So aside from their social value and the community value, I think [libraries] have the key civilizing value too."
Matthew Olshan (p. 31)

"I think of it akin to public broadcasting, public television, and public radio and other resources that we have that are so valuable to our education and identification as humans. I can't imagine not having libraries available to us."
Roscoe Orman (p. 106)

"Books teach the writer to write."
Sterling D. Plumpp (p. 52)

"And truly, even in the modern age, the library offers resources that you can't get in the same way on the Internet."
Matthew Porter (p. 69)

"Maybe some young kids today will start playing games in libraries like I did and be the game designers of tomorrow."
Chris Pramas (p. 128)

"I think the library is invaluable because it is a place that you go to rather than using the computer to bring the information to you."
Dylan Pritchett (p. 72)

"To be able to be in a library and have books readily available and computers to use to find them anywhere was intriguing to me."
Libya Pugh (p. 74)

"The library and the bookstore and the streets and the bars – the saloons, the taverns – they became my curriculum, if you will."
Louis Reyes Rivera (p. 54)

"I know entire school districts, entire counties that don't have librarians staffing elementary schools. That's insane."
Jeff Savage (p. 108)

"But just having that outlet to get a bunch of books... it was almost like visiting a new country or having a new experience. And then it would revive me and I would get back into the groove."
Marc Kelly Smith (p. 57)

"I think you can be inspired for a lifetime by visiting the library."
Dakeyia Sterling (p. 111)

"Most libraries have Internet access or their websites on the Internet. So you can do library research without actually having to go to the library."
David Ufer (p. 33)

"I don't know many writers who don't love to read."
Suzanne Williams (p.35)

"Eventually, I started visiting libraries not to learn about other individuals that were doing what I wanted to do; I started to visit libraries to *do* what those individuals were doing. And that is write plays."
Mike Wiley (p. 77)

The Bookworm, 1850.   Carl Spitzweg

Appendix

Glossary,
Resources,
Acknowledgements
& Index

Sage Ross

Obsolete card catalog files at Sterling Memorial Library, Yale University.

Glossary of Library Terms

academy – Institution of higher education or the faculty of an institution of higher education. A body of learned people. Various associations of scholars, artists, literary men and women, and scientists, organized for the promotion of general or special intellectual or artistic interests, not necessarily connected with any distinct school.

acquisition - Refers to the locating, ordering, purchasing, and receiving of materials in the library collection.

American Library Association - Organization founded in 1876 to influence publishing, lobbying, and education on behalf of librarians. Sets standards in library education and accreditation.

archives – Records considered worthy of permanent preservation. Also designates the agency charged with custody, preservation, and administration of archival material and the building in which archives are housed. The person who administrates the archives is an archivist.

bookmobile - A movable vehicle used as a library. Bookmobiles often provide library services to communities without library buildings.

card catalog - A register of items found in a particular library or group of libraries. Bibliographic items can be novels, computer files (e-books and ejournals, web pages, databases), graphics, maps, or other information resources considered relevant to the library and its users. In most libraries, the card catalog has been replaced by the Online Public Access Catalog (OPAC).

cataloger - A library professional who organizes and provides information about the contents of a book and/or the collection that houses the book.

cataloging – Furnishes information about the content of a library's collection. An item is described in terms of author, title, publisher, date, size, page numbers, and subject. The item is assigned a call number or "address" within the library for later retrieval. Catalogs were once principally typed on 3x5 cards contained in a cabinet. Today, most catalogs are accessible online.

circulation – Those functions that involve lending items to library users guided by defined borrowing policies.

collection development – Librarians decide which items to add to the library collection.

comedy – Deals with the light and amusing side of human existence. Often depicts the follies and absurdities of human beings and it may have a satiric purpose.

database – Electronic information retrieval system not to be confused with the Internet.

Dewey Decimal Classification System – Uses decimal fractions to indicate the subject content of a work. Ten main classes of work are represented by numbers then sub-classes are represented by decimals. The first letter of the last name of the author or the title is included. Allows individual libraries to closely tailor the cataloging of their holdings. This system became outdated as new subjects grew beyond the ten main classes.

essay – Literary form defined as an expository piece of prose. Informs and explains rather than dramatizes and creates. Achieves effect by direct statement rather than using imaginary characters to act out a situation. Usually confined to a particular aspect of a subject from the writer's own point of view.

interlibrary loan – Allows library users to request materials and resources not available in their primary library.

Internet – An international data communication system that allows the exchange of information not to be confused with an online database.

librarian – Provides oversight to the library. Serves in leadership roles administering the organization and subunits. Assumes primary responsibility for providing reference assistance, developing and managing the collections, and overseeing the catalog. Requires bibliographic, technological, communication, and interpersonal skills.

library – A collection of materials organized for use. Libraries function to collect, preserve, organize, and retrieve information for users. Libraries mainly perform acquisition, collection development, cataloging, preservation, reference, and circulation. Types of libraries include academic, government, public, school, and special.

Library of Congress – Established by the federal government in 1800 in Washington, D.C., it is the largest library in the world. Serves the North American national legislature, scholars, researchers, and libraries around the world. It is divided into four major units – Congressional Research Services, the Copyright Office, the Law Library, and Library Services.

Library of Congress Classification System (LC) - Formulated based on the need to organize works acquired by the Library of Congress. Many other libraries use the system however. Twenty-one categories are represented by letters and numbers, then further sub-divided. The call number represents the location of an object on the library shelf just as the number on a house represents its location on the city street. It is an address.

lyric – Short poem that conveys intense personal emotion or thought. Principally a poem that is sung.

non-fiction – A work presented as fact, meaning the work can be proven true or proven false. Essays, journals, documentaries, scientific papers, photographs, biographies, textbooks, and journalism are some examples of non-fiction.

novel – Fictional prose narrative in which characters and situations are depicted within the framework of a plot. Seems as though it could be factual description of actual people and events, but is not.

novella – Fictional work shorter than a novel but longer than a short story.

monograph - A book or a group of books on related subjects that is a one-time publication, complete in itself.

periodical – A type of serial publication that is produced under the same title continuously, regularly (or irregularly), usually numbered and dated with no foreseen conclusion. Magazines, journals, and newspapers are periodicals.

play – Literary composition, in either verse or prose that tells a story through action and speech and is usually intended to be performed by actors before an audience. An element of theater.

poem – Imaginative expression that is essentially metrical or written according to stanzaic forms. As a literary form, poetry is generally synonymous with verse and is contrasted to the conventional prose of exposition, narrative, or argument. Literature that is singular for the affecting sound or imagery of its language.

preservation – Concerns the maintenance and safekeeping of physical and electronic library collections for future use.

primary documentation – A source of information created at or near the time being studied, by an authority with direct knowledge of the events described. Official reports, speeches, pamphlets, posters, or letters, eyewitness accounts, oral interviews (recordings and transcripts), journals, essays, photographs, paintings, and buildings, are forms of primary documentation.

profession – Certain types of skilled work at a recognized standard of ability requiring formal training, or extensive academic study. Professions control the training, evaluation, licensing, certification, ethics, procedures, protocols, and admission of members. Members of professions exercise independent judgement and ethics. Often the required skill sets of a profession are rewarded by payment or salary.

public services – Library functions that provide direct, external service to users including activities such as reference, circulation, inter-library loan, and instruction.

reference - Reference librarians assist people to find the information they need, through a structured conversation called the reference interview. This assistance may consist of research on a specific question, direction on the use of electronic databases; obtaining special material; or providing access to delicate and/or expensive material.

research - Intellectual investigation with the goal of discovery, interpretation, and revision of human knowledge. These efforts may conclude with published results that generate further inquiry in addition to public, corporate, or institutional support.

scholarly sources – Information edited, proofed, and fact-checked by experts and/or professionals in a particular subject field, also known as peer-reviewed.

screenplay – Literary composition, usually prose that tells a story through action and speech and is usually intended to be performed by actors and recorded for mass reproduction.

secondary documentation – A work written based on information gathered from primary sources and other secondary sources. Secondary sources report on past events and provide analysis, synthesis, interpretation, translation, and evaluation.

short story – Work of prose fiction, characterized by brevity and by strictly ordered economy of plot and character.

special library – Serves specific professionals or institutions in narrow subject areas. Includes medical and law, corporate and non-profit, military and prison, and private research libraries.

technical – Having special knowledge of a subject, particularly mechanical or scientific. Relating to a particular practical or scientific subject or mode of training.

technical services – Library functions related to internal operations including acquisition, collection development, cataloging, and preservation.

technology – Applied science. A technical method of achieving a practical purpose.

Resources

About.com Quotation Search Page http://quotations.about.com *Accessed December 15, 2006*

Bartlett's Familiar Quotations. http://www.bartleby.com *Accessed December 15, 2006*

Bartlett's Familiar Quotations. Little, Brown & Company. Boston. 16th ed. 1992

Bartlett's Familiar Quotations. Little, Brown & Company. Boston. 13th ed. 1955

Battles, Matthew. Library: An Unquiet History. W.W. Norton & Company. 2003

Canfield, Jack and Gay Hendricks (eds.). You've Got to Read This Book! 55 People Tell the Story of the Book that Changed Their Life. Harper Collins. 2006.

Coady, Roxanne J. and Joy Johannsessen (eds.). The Book That Changed My Life: 71 Remarkable Writers Celebrate the Books That Matter Most to Them. Gotham Books. 2006

Collier's Encyclopedia. Collier's. New York. 1997

Contemporary Authors Online. The Gale Group. *Accessed December 15, 2006-September 22, 2007*

The Crown Treasury of Relevant Quotations. Crown Publishers, Inc. New York. 1978

Dictionary of Quotations. Delacorte Press. New York. 1968

Funk & Wagnalls New Encyclopedia. Funk & Wagnalls. New York. 1989

Google. http://www.google.com *Accessed December 15, 2006-November 15, 2007*

Hodge, Anthony and Bastiaan F. Zwaan. Risen: Why Libraries Are Here to Stay: The Technology that Almost Took the Library's Power Away is Now Giving it Back. ALA Special Edition. 2007.

The Home Book of Quotations Classical and Modern. Dodd, Mead & Company. 10th ed. 1967

The MacMillan Dictionary of Quotations. MacMillan Publishing Company. New York. 1989

Nickerson, Sheila B. Writers in the Public Library. Library Professional Publications. 1984.

Olmert, Michael. Smithsonian Book of Books. Smithsonian Books. Washington. 1992

The Oxford Dictionary of Quotations. Oxford University Press. New York. 3rd ed. 1979

Simpson's Contemporary Quotations. http://www.bartleby.com *Accessed December 15, 2006*

Marquis Who's Who in America. Reed Publishing, Inc. 2006

Wikipedia. http://www.wikipedia.org *Accessed December 15, 2006-November 15, 2007*

Acknowledgements

Cover
Lee McQueen.

Photographs
Frontispiece. McQueen Press. "Library of Congress."
p. 12, 14, 16, 20, 22, 24, 26, 30, 33, 35, 41, 44, 48, 50, 70, 74, 76, 83, 86, 89, 91, 94, 97, 103, 105, 108, 111, 115, 119, 122, 125, 127. McQueen Press. Used with permission of the subjects, Patrick Carman, Cooper Edens, Phil Foglio, Sheryl McFarlane, Anthony Ellis McGee, Terry Moore, John Nance, Matthew Olshan, David Ufer, Suzanne Williams, Dave Gegic, Quraysh Ali Lansana, Raúl Niño, Sterling D. Plumpp, Dylan Prichett, Libya Pugh, Mike Wiley, Zaid Abdul-Aziz, Jeff Angus, Alan Axelrod, Timuel D. Black, Jr., Claire Buchwald, Anthony Chiffolo, George Norfleet, Roscoe Orman, Jeff Savage, Dackeyia Sterling, Mohammed Aman, John Burgess, Anthony Hodge, and Chris Pramas.
p. 18. Mary Halpin Studios. Used with permission of the subject, J.A. Jance.
p. 39. Fred Viebahn. Used with permission of the photographer, Fred Viebahn, and the subject, Rita Dove.
p. 53. Jenny Lau. Used with permission of the subject, Louis Reyes Rivera.
p. 60. Squirrelist. "Hemingway's Writing Desk in Key West." Used with permission of the photographer, Squirrelist. Wikipedia Commons. Granted to public domain by photographer, Squirrelist, December 2002.
p. 65. Brian McConley. Used with permission of the subject, Kirk Hanley.
p. 68. Matthew Porter. Used with permission of the subject, Matthew Porter.
p. 100. Deborah Triplett. Used with permission of the subject, Rosie Molinary.
p. 125. David Christopher. Used with permission of the subject, Olofunmilayo Olopade.
p. 144. Sage Ross. "Yale Card Catalog." Used with permission of the photographer, Sage Ross. Wikipedia Commons. Granted to public domain by photographer, Sage Ross, April 2006.
p. 160. McQueen Press. Used with permission of the subject, Lee McQueen.

Images
p. iv. Lee McQueen. "Lee's Typewriter." Used with permission of the creator, Lee McQueen.
p. 8. Medieval Writing Desk. Small illustration scanned from the book *Rodwell, G. F.: "South by East: Notes of Travel in Southern Europe" (1877)*. Wikipedia Commons. Public Domain.

p. 11. Mary Sundstrom. "Curse of the ChupaCabra." Used with permission of the publisher, University of New Mexico Press, and the subject, Rudolfo Anaya.

p. 57. Michael Acerra. "Crowdpleaser." Used with permission of the subject, Mark Smith.

p. 60. Yale Collection of American Literature, Beinecke Rare Book and Manuscript Library. "Frontispiece and title page of Phillis Wheatley (1753-1784): *Poems on various subjects, religious and moral.* By Phillis Wheatley, Negro servant to Mr. John Wheatley, of Boston, in New England. London: Printed for A. Bell, bookseller, Aldgate; and sold by Messrs. Cox and Berry, King-street, Boston. 1773." Wikipedia Commons. Public Domain.

p. 63. Lee McQueen. "Black Diamond." Used with permission of the creator, Lee McQueen.

p. 80. Giuseppe Arcimboldo. "The Librarian."1556. Wikipedia Commons. Public Domain.

p. 142. Carl Spitzweg. "The Bookworm." 1850. Wikipedia Commons. Public Domain.

Text

p. 11. Rudolfo Anaya. Original essay written 2006 for *Writer in the Library!* Used with permission of the author, Rudolfo Anaya.

p. 39. Rita Dove. "Maple Valley Branch Library, 1967" *On the Bus with Rosa Parks,* W.W. Norton & Co., Inc., © 1999 by Rita Dove. Reprinted by permission of the author, Rita Dove.

Index

ABC World News, 29
Abdul-Aziz, Zaid, 83-85, 137
academic library, ii, 49, 63, 90, 100-101
academy, ii-iii, 92, 114
actor, 62-63, 74, 77, 106
Adventures of Huckleberry Finn, The, 68
aerospace analyst, 29
Afghanistan, 101, 116
Africa, 117, 45, 55, 72
  South, 51
African American, 22, 45, 47, 55, 57, 64, 70, 72, 76-77, 80, 86, 92, 101-103, 105-107, 118
Afro American
  see African American
Alaska, 27
album, 6
Alice in Wonderland, 65
Aman, Mohammed, 115-118, 137
Amazon.com, 31, 98
American Indian
  see Native American
anatomy, 25
Anaya, Rudolfo, 11, 137
Angus, Jeff, 86-88, 137
anthology, 97
anthropology, 92
archive, 6, 13, 27, 90, 93, 125
Are You Ready For Me?, 95
Arizona, 20
  Bisbee, 18-19
  Tucson, 18
art, 5-6, 16, 23-24, 40, 45-46, 98, 116
artists, 4, 7, 16, 51, 77, 98, 114
Asimov, Isaac, 116
Atlanta Public Library, 90
audio, 7, 28, 78
aviation, 5, 26
Axelrod, Alan, 8, 89-90, 137
Baartman, Saartijie, 64

babysitting, 4, 12
Baldwin, James, 50
Barnes & Noble, 84
Beckham, David, 109-110
Berwyn 57
Bethel, Kathleen, 64
Bible
  See *The Holy Bible*
bibliophile, 120
biography, 42, 74, 78, 106, 116
biology, 41
Black American
  see African American
Black Jr., Timuel D., 3-4, 91-93, 137
Black Hawk Wars, 58
Book of Mornings, A, 49
Book That Changed My Life, The, iii
bookmobile, iii, 20, 53, 89, 103
book-on-tape, 42, 98
bookstore, iii, 4, 7, 19, 42, 54-55, 64-65, 74, 77-78
bookworm, 58, 116
Borders, 74, 84
Bridges of Memory, 92-93
British, 40, 54
Buchwald, Claire, 3, 94-96, 137
Buck, M.W., 41
Buck, Pearl S., 41
Burgess, John, 3, 119-121, 138
business, 5, 7, 58, 67, 119-121
Cairo University, 116
California
  University of, Davis, 119-120
  University of, Los Angeles, 26
call number, 7
card catalog, 5, 49, 86, 95, 122-123
Carman, Patrick, 3, 12-13, 138
Carnegie, Andrew, 28
Carson, Ben, 23

Carter G. Woodson Regional Library, 22, 47, 93

cassette, 6

Catcher in the Rye, The, 84

CD, 6, 17

Champaign-Urbana
  University of Illinois, 92

chap book, 45, 49

chemistry, 25, 41

Chestnut, Charles, 71

Chicago, 57-58, 64, 89, 92-93, 124, 126
  Cultural Center, 4, 52, 57, 91
  Dramatists, 64
  Historical Society, 57
  Public Library, 52, 57, 89, 124, 126
  University of, 92
  University of Illinois, 92

Chief Crazy Horse, 53

Chiffolo, Anthony, 3, 97-99, 138

children, 5, 20, 23, 35, 53, 69, 72-73, 75, 94-95, 98, 105-107, 119, 126

China, 41, 101

classics, 13, 25, 68

Columbia University, 116

Columbus, Christopher, 59

comedy, 65-67

computer, 2, 6, 8, 25, 28, 51, 72-74, 84, 86, 104, 116-117, 126

Contemporary Authors, i

Cooking with the Bible, 98

cookbook, 33

Creel, George, 90

Critica Nueva, 11

Dark Hills Divide, The, 12

Darkness to Sunlight, 83

database, i, 98

DaVinci Code, The, 104

De Soto, Hernando, 59

Devices and Desires, 42

Dewey Decimal System, 27, 66, 74

Diamond, Lydia, 63-64, 138

dictionary, 19, 109, 5

directory, 112

dissertation, 89

Divine Days, 50

documentary 77-78, 82, 93

Domes (Digest of Middle Eastern Studies), 118

Dove, Rita, 39-40, 138

drama, 54, 64, 77, 82

dream, 15, 39, 46, 117

Dunbar, Paul Laurence, 71, 105

DVD, 6, 27

Ebay, 31, 59

Ebscohost, 110

Edens, Cooper, 14-15, 138

education, iii-iv, 7, 21, 24-25, 45, 76, 87, 102, 107, 110, 114, 120, 128

Egypt, 99, 115, 117

eight-track, 6

encyclopedia, i, 5, 16, 53-54, 86

engineering, 5, 120

English, 21, 48, 72, 90, 112, 116, 126

Entertainment Power Players, 112

essay, iii, 82

Europe, 14, 55, 58, 123

evolution, 111

ex-slave narrative, 71-72

fantasy, 4, 13, 15-16, 34, 72, 128

father, 3, 19, 91, 101, 106-107, 126

Faulkner, William, 50

fiction, 10, 13, 16, 22, 25, 27, 30, 33, 36, 42-43, 45, 50, 65, 68, 72, 74, 78, 83, 86, 92, 101-102, 106, 116, 126-128

film, 2, 6-7, 51, 76-78, 112

finance, 36, 66-67, 75, 98

Florida, 68

flower, 15, 36, 39

Foglio, Phil, 16-17, 138

folio, 44

Forestville Public Library, 3, 91

Frankenstein, 13

French, 39, 54, 89

game, 2, 109, 127-128

garden, 4, 15-16

Gegic, David, 41-43, 139

Gehrig, Lou, 108

genre, ii-iv, 64, 112, 128

German, 54
Gifted Hands, 23
Giovanni, Nikki, 63
Giraffe Who Was Afraid of Heights, The, 34
Girl Who Loved Pigeons, The, 84
Godin, Seth, 69
Good Morning, America, 29
Google, 17, 23, 25, 27, 121-122, 128
graphic, 7, 25
Greenway School, 18
handbook, ii, 5
Hall Branch (Library), 91
Hanley, Kirk, 65-67, 139
Harold Washington Library, 52, 126
Harris, E. Lynn, 22
health, 36, 98, 120
Hemingway, Ernest, 115, 117
Hershey, John, 84
hip hop, 51
history, ii, 5, 16, 21, 25, 40, 43-45, 47, 55-56, 66, 75, 77-78, 90, 97-99, 103-106, 115-116, 127-128
Hodge, Anthony, 122-124, 139
Holy Bible, The, 109, 112
Hour of the Hunter, 18
Howard, Ryan, 109
Hughes, Langston, 92, 105
humor, 67, 123
Hyde Park-Kenwood, 92, 126
illustration, 15
illustrator, 7, 14
Indian
  see Native American
information, i, iii-iv, 2, 4-7, 11, 22-23, 31, 43, 47, 66, 68-69, 72, 77, 87, 90-92, 98-99, 104, 106-107, 108-110, 117, 120-124, 126
instant messaging, 19
inter-library loan, 18, 87
Internet, 13, 19, 21-23, 25-27, 31, 34, 36, 42-43, 46, 49, 51, 58, 66, 69, 74, 83-84, 87, 90, 95, 98, 101, 104, 107, 109-110, 112, 116-118, 120-123, 126, 128

Iowa
  State University, 83
  University of, 89
Ipod, 29
Irish, 54
Italy, 95
James, P.D., 42
Jance, J.A., 4, 18-19, 149
Jazz in Jail, The, 55
Johns Hopkins University, 23
Johnson, John H., 23
Jones, Edward P., 84
journal, 20-21, 41, 45-46, 82, 101, 118, 123
Journal of Ordinary Thought, 46
journalism, 82
k-12, 45-46
King, Stephen, 33
King Jr., Martin Luther, 111
Kite Runner, The, 116
Lansana, Quraysh Ali, 44-47, 139
Lawrence of Arabia, 54
Lee, Spike, 51
Leonard, Elmore, 58
Lewis, C. Day, 19
librarian, iii-iv, 4, 12, 16, 20, 28, 30, 35, 40, 44, 53, 63-64, 66, 76, 84-85, 87-88, 100, 109-110, 116-117, 122
library assistant, 122
library card, 40, 42, 46, 53, 65, 70, 94, 105, 110
Library of Congress, 28
library page, 122
Little Mermaid, The, 15
literacy, 21, 102
Long Ago Told, 19
Lorca, Federico García, 50
Lord of the Rings, 13
Los Angeles Times, 109
Lost in the City, 84
Love in the Time of Cholera, 78
lyric, 38, 51
magazine, 7, 23, 27, 33, 36, 39, 42, 45, 69, 76-77, 92, 109, 112
Mandela, Nelson, 51

map, 6, 25

Massachusetts
Amherst, 63
Peabody, 127

Max Talks to Me, 96

McFarlane, Sheryl, 20-21, 139

McGee, Anthony Ellis, 22-23, 139

McMillan, Terry, 22

McQueen, Lee, i-iv, 3-8

medicine, 23

microfilm, 125

Minnesota
Edina, 94

Molinary, Rosie, 100-102, 139

Moore, Terry, 24-25, 139

monograph, 29

Morgan, Helen, 26

Morrison, Toni, 50

mother, ii, 3, 41, 44, 63, 76, 89, 91, 94, 105,116-117, 119

museum, 4, 46

mythology, 16

Nance, John, 26-29, 140

National Geographic, 27

National Institutes of Health, 120

Native American, 47, 53, 55, 58

neighborhood, 7, 15, 46, 53, 65, 76, 91-92

neighborhood library
see public library

Neighborhood Writing Alliance, 46

New Jersey
Burganfield, 33

New Mexico
Public Library, 11
University of, 11

New York, 45
Bedford-Stuyvescent, 83
Bronx, The, 105
Brooklyn, 83
Times, 109

newspaper, ii, 6, 13, 21, 78, 109

Niño, Raúl, 48-49, 140

non-fiction, iii-iv, 20, 26-27, 36, 41, 45, 65-66, 74-75, 77-78, 82, 86, 90, 101, 106, 109

Norfleet, George, 103-104, 140

Northwestern University, 64
Library, 63

novel, 10-11, 13, 20, 25, 54, 58, 64, 66, 71, 78, 92, 98, 128

Oak Park Public Library, 42, 57

Oklahoma, 47

Olopade, Olofunmilayo, 3, 125-126, 140

Olshan, Matthew, 30-32, 140

On the Road, 68

Oprah Winfrey Show, The, 78

oral history, 78

Orbit, 29

Oregon
Eugene, 35

Orman, Roscoe, 3, 105-107, 140

Palm, 117

parent, 4, 21, 35, 41, 64, 98, 139

Parks, Rosa, 111

PDF, 126

Peckinpah, Sam, 51

permission, 41, 85

Pets From the Pond, 41

Philadelphia Phillies, 109

Phoenix Public Library, 122

photograph, 48, 51, 82, 84, 98

photographer, 7, 98

photography, 5

physics, 125

Pittsburgh, University of, 116-117

play, iii, 62, 64, 74-75, 77-79

playwright, 77

Plumpp, Sterling D., 50-52, 140

poem, 38, 45, 51-52, 55-56, 111

poet, 50-52, 54, 105

poetry, iii, 19, 38, 40-42, 45, 47-48, 55-56, 58, 105

poison, 25, 40

political science, 123

Porter, Matthew, 68-69, 140

Powell, Colin, 42

Pramas, Chris, 127-128, 141
Pratchett, Terry, 126
pre-Columbian, 40, 58
Premiere, 77
Premio Aztlan, 11
Primary Colors, 78
Pritchett, Dylan, 70-73, 141
public affairs, 123
public broadcasting, 106
public education, 13, 46 128
public library, 12, 21, 35-36, 55, 57, 78, 87, 90, 93, 106, 108-109, 115, 117, 122-123, 126
public school
    see public education
Pugh, Libya, 74-75, 141
Purple Cow, 69
rap, 51
religion, 5, 71, 98
research, i-ii, 5-6, 13, 22, 24-26, 29, 34, 46-47, 49, 54, 56-58, 63-64, 67, 71-72, 76, 78, 84, 92-93, 95, 97-98, 100-101, 104, 107-109, 112, 118-122, 125, 127
Rice, Anne, 33
Risen: Why Libraries are Here to Stay, 6, 123
Rivera, Louis Reyes, 53-56, 141
Rolling Stone, 77
Russian, 54
Ruth, Babe, 108
Sacco and Vanzetti Trial, 97
saint, 97-98
Saint Louis University, 97
Savage, Jeff, 108-110, 141
Scattered Scripture, 56
Schomburg Center, 45-46
school, iv, 3, 8, 13, 16, 18, 30, 35-36, 40, 44, 46, 48, 50, 53-54, 57, 63-64, 86, 89, 91-92, 97-98, 103, 105, 108, 109-111, 114, 122, 125
school library, 28, 48, 65, 109, 125
science, 13, 16, 25, 33, 41-43, 69, 83, 104, 114, 116-117, 120, 126-128
screenplay, 62, 66

scripture, 98-99
Sea Stories, 15
Seattle Public Library, 84, 87
Shoreline Library, 83, 85
short story, 10
Sinbad the Sailor, 15
slave narrative
    see ex-slave narrative
Smith, Marc Kelly, 57-59, 141
software, 120
Somehow We Survive, 51
sport, 5, 108, 112
Sports Illustrated, 118
statistic, 21
Sterling, Dackeyia, 111-112, 141
Strawberry Girl, 35
Streeter, Captain, 58
style guide, 5
Succeeding Against the Odds, 23
Tanzania, 118
tax, 6, 36
technical, iii, 41, 68, 114
technology, ii, 25, 50, 93, 114, 120
television, 2, 66, 106, 112
theater, 62-65, 67, 98, 105
thesaurus, 25, 109
They Shall Run-Harriet Tubman Poems, 44
Tohono O'otham, 18
Tolstoy, Leo, 115
Transcendentalists, 54
translation, 98-99, 115
Treasury of the Familiar, 19
Tubman, Harriet, 45-46
Turn of the Screw, 13
Twain, Mark, 57
Tyree, Omar, 22
Ufer, David, 33-34, 141
Underground Railroad, 45-46
university library
    see academic library
V for Victory, 128
Velvet BeBop: Kente Cloth, 51
video, 6, 28, 78, 98
Virginia, 64, 70, 76, 104

Vivian Harsh Collection, 47, 93
Voyeurs de Venus, 64
Walker, Alice, 50, 126
War and Peace, 115
Washington (State), 85
   Seattle, 87
   Tacoma, 27
   Walla Walla, 12
Washington, D.C., I, 30, 84, 104
Washington, Denzel, 77
Wheatley, Phyllis, 111
Where the Sidewalk Ends, 19
White Lotus, 84
Who's Who in America, i
Wikipedia, i

Wild Bunch, The, 51
Wildwood School, 63
Wiley, Mike, 76-79, 141
Williams, Robin, 77
Williams, Suzanne, 35-36, 141
Woods, Tiger, 103
word-processing, 83
World is Flat, The, 69
World War I, 90
World Wide Web, 109
Wright, Karavill, 18-19
Writer in the Public Library, iii
You've Got to Read this Book!, iii
Zimmerman Library, 11

About the Author

Lee McQueen has a Master of Library and Information Science from SUNY-Buffalo and a Bachelor of Arts in Political Science from Xavier University of Louisiana. She has been both a librarian and a bookstore owner. Now editor and publisher at McQueen Press, she also takes on indexing and abstracting, database maintenance, proofreading, and research and writing assignments. In the past, she's written the poetry book, *Things I Forgot to Tell You*, the screenplays, *The Angel and the Lion* and *Kindred*, the short story collection, *Imaginarium*, and the novel, *Kenzi*. In addition, she's written research articles for Scribner Group, political essays for various public affairs outlets, and book reviews for *Library Journal*. Forthcoming are another short story collection, *The Dark Fantastic*, and the novel, *Jeannie East then West*.

McQueen Press
welcomes your comments on
Writer in the Library! and
your own writer/library
experiences at

www.mcqueenpress.com/blog.html

Thank you for reading!

And writing!

www.ingramcontent.com/pod-product-compliance
Lightning Source LLC
Chambersburg PA
CBHW050946120626
46552CB00001B/399